GOING SOUTH

WITH THE GOD OF JACOB'S AND MY
MISTAKES

MARCIA MOSTON

Edie –
With thanks for the myriad
of ways you help others
tell their stories
me included.

Marcia

To Eileen, my prayer warrior sister who, instead of judging or condemning me when I unknowingly drank her Bible group's communion wine, prayed me into the kingdom.

and

In memory of Pastor Bill Chadwick—Billy to me—who's now probably heading up the Department of Humor and Outrageous Fun after riding his Harley into glory with that perpetual grin on his face.

YOU KNOW you're in trouble when you look for encouragement from the story of someone remembered more for the predicaments he got himself into than for his commendable deeds. But like Jacob, some of us have to wrestle an angel of the Lord all night before we get to the end of ourselves and trust that the Lord can and will orchestrate all he's appointed for us, in spite of us—even when we make bad decisions and big mistakes. Like the one I made when my husband, trusting my previously sound judgment, agreed to let me go ahead south and pick out our house while he stayed up north to finish work. It was supposed to be our final house—the low-maintenance, efficient one. I wanted a pool. Bob wanted a garage. It was a good plan. I should have stuck to it.

CONTENTS

PART I

CHOICES

We put so much pressure on ourselves, as if the eternal plans of the almighty God are contingent on our ability to decipher them. —Mark Batterson

DOOR ON THE LEFT? DOOR ON THE RIGHT?

YEARS ago I unwittingly sent my junior high literature students into fits of frustration with the assignment to write an ending to "The Lady or the Tiger," a short story by Frank Stockton. In it a barbarian king learns his daughter has a lover who is beneath her royal status. The king subjects the lover to a trial in a public arena. He stands before two doors. Behind one is a ferocious tiger; behind the other is a woman he must marry on the spot. As the star-crossed lover is to choose, he glances at his princess in the stands. She has discovered what is behind each door and gives him a signal.

We wonder—Is her love pure enough to let him live, even if it means with another woman? Or does she have a jealous, barbaric heart that would prefer him dead? And, most important to the lover, does he know his princess well enough to interpret her signal? At the moment of decision, when my kids are flipping the page to see which door the unfortunate man is going to choose, the author, Frank Stockton, ends with, "And so I leave it with all of you: Which came out of the opened door—the lady, or the tiger?"

The class goes into an uproar—groans, books slamming shut. Even the kids who usually find it more fascinating to string paperclip sculptures through literature class sit up, wide-eyed in disbelief that an author would leave his readers hanging. But my students weren't the only ones wanting to scream at the conclusion. Readers from all over the world bombarded Stockton with demands for the answer. "Tell us—Which door?"

I sympathize. How many times have I stood before my own two doors and wondered which to choose? How many times have I begged God to tell me what to do, where to go? I know God isn't an unreliable lover like the princess in the story, or as the prophet Jeremiah laments, a deceptive stream that runs in the wet season and disappears in the dry (Jeremiah 15:18). But I have to admit, sometimes I'm impatient with his seemingly unhurried interest in answering. Doesn't he realize I'm in a crisis and need an answer *now*. Sometimes it seems so uncertain to wait for the Lord. Other times I don't trust myself to hear his response. What if I make a bad, or selfish, or rash decision? I know he works all things to the good in the spiritual realm, but what about the repercussions in the physical realm? What if it costs me more than I expected? And more times than I care to admit—I want what I want, but I want God to sign off on it with his Good Housekeeping Seal of approval, guaranteeing that it will work out well for me.

Regardless how we approach them, unless there's been some unforeseen resolution—all the other choices fall through or God intervenes in a miraculous way—sooner or later, most decisions come to this:

Door on the left? Door on the right?

Time's up. Choose.

WE THROW A DART AT A MAP AND CHOOSE

I HOISTED MY CARRYON, relieved that it slid into the slender space of the overhead and I didn't have to hold up the long line of passengers boarding behind me while I jostled to fit it in. The last time I'd flown without my husband, my seat had been three-quarters of the way to the back, and there were no empty bins by the time I got there. A frazzled flight attendant had leaned around the several heads separating us and told me to take my bag up front and check it, something I would have gladly done if it didn't mean swimming against the current of impatient people between the door and me. I just stood there, paralyzed by the impossibility until someone got up, rearranged the luggage in the overhead, and stored my bag for me.

This time, without the pressure of bulky baggage, I sat down and belted up. Armed with a batch of real estate listings and my husband's faith in my house-buying judgment, I was flying to Greenville, SC, a place I'd never been, but one that would soon, like ink on a blotter, seep into and color every corner of the next years of our lives.

After takeoff, when all the sighings and settlings—the click of briefcase latches, rustle of magazines, and squeak of pushed back seats—quieted, the woman next to me looked over at the stack of printouts I had on my lap and asked if I were moving to Greenville. Her husband was a realtor in a nearby town and she knew the area well.

I said we were. "But our home sold faster than we expected, and we've been living in an inn for the past month. My husband's tied up with work so I'm going on ahead to find us a house." I picked up the first listing of a simple brick ranch. "We're not retiring yet, but we want to downsize. We've already renovated four houses. This time we want something we can buy outright—efficient, low-maintenance—so we can be in a good position for the next season of our lives. Bob wants a garage or workshop and I have to have a swimming pool." I handed her the spec sheet. "I can't get over how much less expensive houses are there than in the North."

She scanned the description. Although the change in her expression was subtle, within a nanosecond, I perceived a whole conversation had passed across her face before it rearranged itself into a wary smile. With a simple syllable, "Hmm," she nodded, wished me well, and settled back into her seat.

Her response, though quick and guarded, flashed brighter than a warning sign on a dark night: rough road ahead, steep hill, bump. I thumbed through the other listings. Many of them were clustered in the same zip code—probably a clue as to why they were so inexpensive. That was the problem with not being familiar with an area. Except for passing through on the interstate at 70 mph, the only thing I knew about where we'd chosen to relocate was what I'd found on internet searches.

Filmy clouds floated past the porthole of a window revealing fields of green thousands of feet below. We were probably flying over one of the Mid-Atlantic States—those buffer zones between the North and the South, between my past and my future. I leaned back in my seat. It was both thrilling and scary to be moving to an unfamiliar place, a place where we neither knew anyone, nor had jobs or any particular reason to be there. But we'd gone to foreign places before. After all, we were the same two who'd packed up their ten-year-old daughter and three trunks' worth of possessions and drove from New Jersey to Guatemala to work in a Mayan orphanage several years ago. The same two who left the security of Bob's well-paying union job in New York City to pastor a small church in Vermont.

Although now we didn't have as defined a purpose nor as much of a plan, it wasn't as though we'd decided on this move impetuously, like twenty-something-year-olds flipping a coin to see where to go next on our backpacking trek across Tibet. We'd been thinking about this ever since that night driving home from a Thanksgiving holiday in Maine. That night when we'd made the initial decision that sent the dominoes of our life tumbling and everything familiar scattering.

Headlights from passing cars on the Maine Turnpike slid across Bob's face, shadowing him in flickers of light and dark. Neither of us had spoken in a while, both occupied by a thought that sat between us as substantial as a third passenger. The idea that our time in Vermont was over had been lurking at the edges of our minds for weeks, but we were stuck in that indecisive space, torn between the frustration of staying and the fear of going.

The problem was that the Lord wasn't showing us what to do or where to go next. No pillar of fire by night or cloud by day. Just the sense that it was time for something else. The future lay before us, a vast, empty plain. If there were one perfect choice, one road that led to the bull's-eye of God's plan for our life, it blurred in the haze of the horizon.

Eleven years earlier Bob had been invited to pastor a little Vermont church, which after over one hundred fifty years of worship, Sunday school lessons, and community potluck dinners, had dwindled down to its last few families. This tenacious remnant hung on without a permanent pastor for over a year. In a step of faith, they pledged to cobble together a modest salary if Bob would leave his job in New York City and help rebuild their church. The offer included the four-room-first floor of the parsonage, an old clapboarded New England home, which was partitioned into two apartments.

The townspeople were duly proud of their brick church, built in 1824 and listed on the National Register of Historic Places. Spittoons that once held functional places at the end of rows of pews now held places of honor behind glass cases in the entryway. Antique organs, whether they worked or not, anchored the sanctuary corners. Membership rolls were long; attendance was short. But the sense of community, history, and tradition ran deep. Townspeople who never stepped out on a Sunday morning showed up for the annual Strawberry Festival and fund-raising potluck dinners on Saturday nights. Having come from the city, we were unfamiliar with such a context, but the faithful core made the commitment to do whatever it took to have a pastor come on board permanently. In our own step of faith, we'd said yes. Bob left his lucrative job in the electrical union; we sold our colonial home in New Jersey, packed our lives in a Penske truck, and moved to Vermont.

It was an unlikely union—Bob, a type-A New Yorker, used to independent, contemporary praise and worship and Bible-preaching churches, now the leader of a tiny, tradition-loving, hymn-singing New England Congregational flock. The relationship, variable as a Vermont day—balmy and peaceful one minute, stormy and cloudy the next—stimulated a lot of grace growing on both sides of the pulpit over the years.

Although Bob had received his degree in pastoral studies, he had never pastored a church before. It was also an unlikely position for me. I had never been a pastor's wife. Not only did I not sing, play the piano, or have a recipe box full of potluck possibilities, but I also didn't have the kind of background that I thought a proper pastor's wife should have.

So when a local paper wanted to do an article on Bob shortly after we arrived, I said, "Maybe you shouldn't tell them who your wife is." I was originally from Vermont and Vermont is a small place. I imagined the shock some of my former friends would have if they read I was back in town as a pastor's wife. Although I ended high school with some laudable achievements that had earned space in the local paper, I'd quickly traded the good Catholic girl of my youth for a "liberated" and rebellious woman coming of age in the aftermath of the '60s. I looked for truth in a lot of wrong places and lived in a lot strange places—like the huge tepee I'd sewn together from pre-cut canvas and set up on a mountainside. (Years later my son, who was applying for a job with a three-letter-name government agency that required a deep background check, joked about how to include the address for a mountainside tepee.)

Nevertheless, over the years Bob and I came to love our church family, and the ones who stayed loved us in return. We knew who had triumphed through a personal difficulty and who hadn't. We cried with young parents in early morning hospital rooms over the death of their child and with elderly widows at gravesides over the loss of their spouses. Bob had married and buried dozens of people. He had prayed with men, women, and children to know Christ, and baptized them in local lakes so they could say it was so.

But the constant ebb and flow of attendance, plus the frustration of leading a congregation divided between traditional ways of worship and the newer relational approaches to God had taken its toll on us. We thought the church needed new energy—energy we didn't have. As sure as we were that God had put us there, now, eleven years later, we believed he was relieving us. We told each other we'd decide after we saw whether or not the congregation passed the budget at the annual October business meeting. That had taken place a few weeks earlier. They hadn't.

I turned to Bob in the darkened car and voiced what we already suspected. "It's over."

He nodded slowly as the weight of the decision settled over him. We drove on into the night, each silently listening to our own thoughts and the hum of tires on a highway.

It was one thing to know we were leaving but another to know where we were going. Having no particular reason to choose one place over another, we could have just as well thrown a dart at a map of the United States. Our children were grown and scattered around the country. Our friends were staying put in the North. Although we didn't know what we'd do for work, we had skills, degrees, and enough money to tide ourselves over until we found jobs, wherever we lived—or so we thought. Resolutely we spread a map before us and listed our priorities: east coast, access to mountains and lakes, culturally alive community, vigorous job market. And sunshine. I don't know if I was beginning to suffer from SAD, seasonal affective disorder, or had just reached an age when all things gray, especially days, got me down. Although blessed with rolling green mountains, vibrant fall foliage, and sugar maple trees, Vermont reportedly rivaled Washington as the state with the fewest number of clear days a year, even fewer than Alaska. After living in Vermont for the past decade, I needed light, lots of light. And that meant going south.

A three-foot-deep February snowfall motivated us to take advantage of the midwinter vacation from school and check out some of the places on our list. We started with Augusta, Georgia. To be fair, it was a cold, wet, dreary afternoon when we arrived in Augusta, which may have accounted for why there were hardly any people out. It looked as though we'd driven onto an abandoned movie set. Thinking we must have misread our directions, we spent another hour of uneventful exploration before going back to the hotel. "I give it a five," I said. Bob is more generous by nature. "I give it a seven." Averaging out with a six, as far as February appearances went, Augusta wasn't looking too good, but we agreed to stay through the weekend. By Sunday we had made up our minds. The sermon at a church we attended was all we needed to spur us on: "God is in charge of your future, don't fear change." I drew a line through Augusta and unfolded the map.

We decided to take a rural route toward Athens, Georgia—rural being the operative word—as we passed restaurants sporting names like the 2 Gun Café and farther up the road, the Possum Café. Arriving in Athens, we followed signs for the Visitors Bureau that led us down tree-lined streets that looped uphill and down, past grand old Victorian and antebellum buildings, sidewalk cafes, statues, and gardens. The city was old. It was new. It was quintessential South meets New England. We liked it. We collected some real estate and things-to-do brochures and decided to stay a few days to get the pulse of the place.

Although Bob was a pro-football fan, solidly behind the New England Patriots, he had never gotten into college football. But we were soon to learn college football was as much a part of the South as shrimp and grits, Sunday morning sermons, and Prohibition moonshine. Being the hometown of the University of Georgia, Athens vibrated with the energy of a Rose Bowl locker room.

A few days later, like the couples in the last scene of the TV show *House Hunters*, we sat in one of the city's numerous cafes and pored over eclectic menus as we discussed our options and cast our votes. "Athens is alive. I give it an eight and a half," I said.

Still more generous, Bob cast his vote. "Nine." We looked at each other. Was this it? If so, why were we both hesitating? Bob put his finger on the problem. "But I don't think we want a Southern college town at this time of our lives."

I agreed and crossed Athens off our list. By now it was time to get back to Vermont, yet we still had no idea where we would be moving. Leaving Athens behind, Bob headed east on the highway.

My eyes glazed as I watched the city disappear out the window. "Lord," I sighed, unable to say more. Signs whizzed past. Suddenly a billboard loomed into view: "Want to talk? —God." A few miles later another billboard: "Need Direction? —God."

Sometimes you can't help but take these things personally. Ha! I do, indeed, Lord. Hadn't thought to seek you on a billboard, but once again I'm asking, what should we do? Where should we go?

The tune on my cell phone interrupted my thoughts. Jannie, my sister who lives in North Carolina, had been following our journey with great interest. She's the kind of person who knows something about everything—the one who'd know Alaska is the only state that can be typed on one row of keys, or that the folds in a chef's toque, or hat, are said to represent the many ways to cook an egg. She's the one you'd want on your team if you were playing Trivia Pursuit. So of course, she'd know the place that fit our criteria.

"Hey, I was looking at some information on event planning and I came across this article about Greenville, South Carolina. It's a great little city with all kinds of things going on. You should check it out."

It was too late to do more than drive through the outskirts at that point on our trip, but I purposed to look into it when we got home. Days later, back in Vermont, I Googled Greenville, compared number of days of sunshine—reportedly sixty more than where I lived—cost of living, housing market, and taxes. Night after night, I scrolled through pictures and descriptions of houses for sale within our price range.

Bob and I looked at all our diplomas on the office wall, certifying us as masters of something—me in religious education, Bob in pastoral ministry. He was also a journeyman electrician with twenty years of experience in a New York City electrical union. "Surely, we'll get jobs," he ventured, glass-half-full optimist he was. But lurking beneath our bravado was the concern that this time we were different—too young to retire, too old to include dates on resumes. Restless to settle the issue of where we were going to live, we decided it was time to choose.

Door on the left? Door on the right? We held our breath and threw. The dart stuck in Greenville.

PART II

GOING SOUTH

No matter where you go, there you are. —*Yogi Berra*

THE SWIMMING POOL CAME WITH A HOUSE

THE YOUNG REAL estate agent assigned to me scrolled through the listings on his computer screen yet again. I had to hand it to him—whether it was because he had the die-hard spirit of a Clemson College football fan or that of an eager newbie real estate agent didn't matter. He'd been downright sporting to show me dozens of houses in one day. I vetoed most of them before he'd even stopped the car—too close to neighbors, to electrical lines, to run-down neighborhoods. No pool. No garage.

Another agent sitting at a nearby desk marveled at how many places we'd looked at. "I would have shown you three," he said. And I would have been out of there in a heartbeat. I knew what I wanted; we just hadn't found it yet. But the clock was ticking; I would be in town for only a few more days.

"Did you see this?" The office manager stood in the doorway. She handed me a copy of a turn-of-the-century bungalow. "It's cute. Nice neighborhood, right around the corner from where I live. And it has a pool." Then, as if an incidental afterthought, "Does need work, though."

I stared at the grainy image on the spec sheet. The

sloping sides of the hip roof and the unwieldy azaleas bordering the wrap-around porch intimated a Southern belle from times past. It certainly wasn't a simple ranch, and I didn't see any sign of a garage. But there, in the background, I could see a gazebo—and an in-ground pool. A quick phone call to set up the appointment and we were on our way.

The realtor retrieved the key from the lockbox, and we stepped inside. The door swung open into a large entryway with narrow doorways heading off in all directions. Heavy curtains and blinds blocked what light managed to get past the low porch roofline. Stained carpeting flowed up the steep, narrow stairs. Yellowed tiles from the hung ceiling covered most of the original beadboard ceilings. We wandered from room to room, following the unmistakable odor of cat urine to a small bathroom. Apparently the family felines had their own room. Mounds of damp kitty litter overflowed a box and clogged the floor register. Quickly pulling the door shut, we moved to the bedroom, the only room where the high ceiling was exposed and the walls were painted instead of being covered in layers of floral wallpaper.

"Well, it has possibilities," my agent offered. "There's probably hardwood under the carpeting. You could open up some of these doorways and pull down the rest of the drop-tiles. The ceilings must be ten feet high." We made one more pass through the house. It was big. It was old. It was dark. And it was definitely not low-maintenance.

I stepped out onto the back deck. The sunlight shimmering off water as blue as a tropical lagoon warmed my vitamin D-deficient flesh, beguiled my senses, and befuddled my judgment. As if they knew I were coming, the owners, having to choose where to put their repair dollars, had chosen to refurbish the pool instead of updating the house. I learned they were talked into renovating the pool because it had been in a terrible state. "The stuff monster movies are made of," the pool lady later told me. "Dead animals. Green so thick trees were growing in it. The crew had HAZMAT suits on."

Most people looking to simplify their lives would have fled a house renovation of such gargantuan proportions, but as I looked at that private backyard, the only things I saw were candlelight dinners in the gazebo and sultry afternoon swims in the pool. And who knew, with all that ambiance maybe I'd be inspired to tackle a dream I had about writing a book.

Warning bells unheeded, I dismissed the cat-urine soaked carpeting and nicotine-stained wallpaper. I ignored the yellow duct tape holding the backdoor trim together. Although I knew we said we were finished with renovations, my penchant for making ugly things beautiful, energized by thirty-six feet of a newly refurbished, dazzling pool in the backyard, overruled my usually sensible nature.

I turned to the realtor. "We'll take it." And with that I contracted to buy a swimming pool with a house attached.

The next day, I flew back to Vermont. Bob studied the few pictures I had. The house did look good on the outside. "It doesn't actually have a garage," I said. "But the back porch is large and screened with plenty of room for your tools, and it has a walk-in crawl space. I looked at a gazillion houses. This was the only one we can afford that has a private yard, character, and a pool."

Ah, daughter of Eve. Following in my distant mother's footsteps, I handed Bob the offering of the lust of my eyes. "We're enterprising; a little remodeling and we can easily make it beautiful," I promised.

The cluster of friends who'd come to help us load the moving truck stood in front of the metal storage unit, now empty as a raided tomb. "That's it." Tom pulled down the door of the Penske van. We eyed the small pile of items left on the pavement and shrugged. If Tom couldn't fit them in, no one could. But it didn't matter. Jettisoning things from the past was just a necessary part of embarking on a new venture.

Kathy handed me a bag of her secret-recipe scones. Shannon loaded us up with enough chocolate to fuel the next fifteen hours. Carol eyed our CRV on the car carrier, hitched behind. She clutched a tiny pill in her hand and extended it to me. "You're sure you don't want a little something for your nerves? It's very mild." I gave her a hug, climbed into the cab, and hoped I wouldn't regret passing on the offer.

As challenging as some of the times had been here, they were also some of the best, most meaningful of our lives. We'd shared everything from meltdowns on mission fields to murder mystery dinners with these people. From kids' baseball games and boyfriends to their baptisms. Sometimes church leadership positions can be a lonely post, but as I waved goodbye to these special couples who were seeing us off, I realized how fortunate we were to have had such good friends.

Decades earlier, when I was in my searching-for-truth era at a transcendental meditation retreat, I heard a Hindu yogi say, "When you're leaving the garden and entering the house, don't look back at the garden; look forward to entering the house." That sounded profound at the time, but now, suspended in that space between yesterday and tomorrow, the familiar and the foreign, I didn't know where to look. I raised my hand to my lips and blew a kiss out the side window to my faithful friends, then faced front.

Bob put the truck into gear. Like a giant snail on the move, we headed out, carrying everything we owned in the vast cargo area behind the cab. As the sun lowered itself behind Adirondacks on that balmy September evening, two months before the first Vermont snowfall, we turned southward out of Rutland, blissfully unaware our plans were about to go south too.

Since we'd had a late start, we agreed to drive five or six hours and then find a motel that had enough space to park so we wouldn't get stuck not being able to back up or turn around. Around midnight we stopped short of the Mason-Dixon Line in a town in Pennsylvania where we'd spend our last night as Northerners. The next day the sun rose bright and cheery. We munched on scones and speculated what life would be like in the South. In spite of our conviviality, the closer we got to South Carolina, the more I worried what Bob would think about the house he'd trusted me to pick out.

After fifteen hours of driving, we arrived at the place that would define the next leg of our life journey. Bob eased the truck into the narrow driveway that straddled a deep culvert. This was his first real-time view of his new home. I watched him carefully. We didn't have much time before the closing to inspect the condition the sellers had left it in. There was no turning back now. The tidy vinyl siding made a good first impression. "Vinyl's final," I quipped.

But that was as far as it went. Like ghosts escaping a graveyard, waves of pent up odors rushed past as we forced open the front door. I wasn't sure if it was dismay or downright horror that crept across Bob's face as his eyes shifted from one forlorn room to another. One thing was certain —he wasn't seeing lazy afternoons with sweet tea by the pool. Although the building inspection report had noted several problems, we thought they were manageable as long as the house was structurally sound. Now I could see Bob wasn't sure. It wasn't what he said, but what he wasn't saying that worried me. I imagined his guardian angel was covering its face under its wing in unbearable sympathy as Bob tried to assess what had possessed his wife to buy a place that he instantly realized was about to suck our time, energy, and life savings into the void of its decrepit interior. No wonder the owner would cry at the closing and thank us for buying it. Suddenly I wanted to cry, too.

FOR BETTER OR FOR WORSE

THAT PART in our marriage vows where we promised "to have and to hold, for better or for worse," came in pretty handy in the ensuing days. I was grateful Bob never blamed me for the position we were in, to say nothing of the fact that screened in or not, a back porch was no garage. But no matter how hot, tired, and frustrated we were, we purposed not to take it out on each other. This was particularly important because for the next several weeks, unless we counted the cashiers at Home Depot and Target, we were our only friends.

We ripped out hundreds of feet of soiled carpeting. When we pulled down the smudgy drop-ceiling tiles, instead of baring lovely, old, ten-foot-high ceilings, we discovered warped and water-stained beadboard, some dingy white, some painted blue. At the end of our second week, I wrote in my journal, *We are near despair. Lord, give me eyes to see the potential beauty behind this disgusting mess. Raise from these ancient ruins, once again, joy and beauty, and well-being.*

Quickly realizing this was going to cost far more than we planned, we needed to do as much of the work ourselves as we could; however, the ceilings were so high I didn't know how we'd be able to lift the drywall. On one of my daily runs to Home Depot, I trailed a truck covered with home improvement signage. I scribbled the contractor's phone number on my shopping list and within minutes I had him on the line. Much to my relief, he was reasonably priced and able to work immediately.

He did a beautiful job installing, taping, and mudding the Sheetrock on the ceiling in the living room, but when his scaffolding punched through a section of dry-rotted floor in the dining room, we learned more dismal news— all the flooring would have to be replaced. Since each ceiling and floor opened onto another, it was impossible to work one room at a time. Within weeks, the whole downstairs was in an upheaval of plaster dust, soggy wallpaper, and ancient, splintery studs.

Each night we fled to our bedroom, the only place that had any semblance of order. Desperate for a reminder of beauty, I painted the ten-foot-high ceiling teal, the color of a ceiling in a room at a resort in Huatulco, Mexico, where we had once spent several blissful days. At least when we lay in bed at night, we could stare at the ceiling and conjure up pleasant memories. As old as the house was, it hadn't offered up any left-behind treasures. The only item of interest was an antique chandelier hanging above the bed. It had five arms branching out from a cylindrical center. Bob speculated it'd make a great place to hide small valuables. Each night he lay in bed and fantasized the chandelier contained the hidden treasures of a previous owner. Surely somewhere in this big old house there must be something of value Bob said.

So far we hadn't found it.

Like an ill-mannered pooch at a chicken-laden table, the renovation gulped its allocated funds and then ate its way through the money we intended to live on until we got settled. Stuck between the proverbial rock and a hard place, unable to leave things as they were, we had no choice but to continue on. I'd underestimated how much our previous renovations had succeeded because of the skilled contributions and advice of friends. Although we had a few acquaintances from churches we'd been visiting here, we didn't know anyone well enough to ask for help carrying four-by-eight-foot sheets of flooring and drywall. Except for our nephew Brian, who'd come down from NC to help us unload the moving van, our son Scott, who came down from DC to lend a hand and a much-needed dose of encouragement, and the sheet rocker I'd stalked down the highway, we had no one to help. Progress was slow and laborious. I was good with the ideas, but Bob was the one who had to do a lot of the actual construction, even though he was an electrician, not a carpenter. But no matter how complex the project, I knew I could count on Bob to figure out how to do it. It was something I'd discovered about him just before we were married.

At the time we had so little money we hadn't even bought wedding rings. We met with the pastor to go over the order of the simple marriage ceremony. All was going well until we came to the exchanging of the vows part. The pastor turned to Bob, "As you slip the ring on her finger, you'll repeat after me. With this ring I do thee wed."

"We don't have rings," Bob said. "We'll have to skip that part."

In memory, I see the pastor with his silver-haired crew cut, standing there, mouth agape. In the lifetime of his officiating wedding ceremonies, he had never had one where the couples didn't exchange rings. How did we expect to say our vows? Having recently come out from a counter-culture lifestyle, I didn't realize what an important part of the wedding ceremony exchanging rings was, especially in the tradition of this church. We tried to convince the distressed pastor it was all right. We'd get them later we said. Reluctantly he agreed to continue, although I suspected he already thought this marriage was off to a rocky start, and our cavalier attitude about wedding rings only confirmed it.

Although I didn't mind waiting to get rings, I wasn't aware of how concerned Bob was.

He came over to my house after work one evening, looking very pleased with himself. He held out his closed fist. "Try this on." I stared at the smooth, chunky, yellow ring nested in the center of his palm.

"I made it," Bob said. "From a brass nut."

I was mortified.

It was so thick that when I slid it on, it forced my pinkie and middle finger apart as if to take a solo center-stage bow. If it were worth its weight in gold, I'd be sporting diamonds too. Although Bob had spent hours grinding and polishing the edges and inner rings, I had no appreciation of his labor of love or his quirky creativity. How could I show off my wedding ring—everyone would know it was brass! Poor but proud, I chose to have no wedding band at all rather than a brass-nut one.

Oh for a life do-over moment. Whenever I look at the fancy gold wedding band that now graces my finger, how I wish I were seeing that brass-nut ring.

Despite Bob's ability and ingenuity, the dreadful realization we were now over our heads stared us in the eye at three in the morning. It ate with us on paper plates of take-out. It sucked our joy, our strength, and our vision. Conflicting entries like the self-accusatory *Macbeth has killed sleep. Marcia has killed sleep*, riddled my journal. And then, indicative of the mental warfare going on, I'd counter with biblical reminders like "The steadfast of mind Thou will keep in perfect peace because he trusts in Thee" (Isaiah 26:3) and "When you lie down, you will not be afraid; When you lie down, your sleep will be sweet" (Proverbs 3:24).

Before long we were left wondering if instead of running strong to the finish line of our lives, we would be crawling across it, covered in Sheetrock dust and regrets. There was no doubt the Lord ultimately works "all things to the good," but until then? I knew he redeemed my life, but would he redeem my mistakes before our money, energy, and hope ran out?

Various trades and utilities people marched through, each gravely handing over their verdicts along with their estimates. Everyone who came in our door eyed the remnants of ancient bark still clinging to the now-exposed wall studs, and the worn, rotted flooring, then said the same three things: "Wow, you have a lot of work to do. It's going to be beautiful when you are through." And then incredulously, "Are you living here?"

Yes, we said, we were.

THE LADY AT THE DOOR

ONE AFTERNOON A CAR pulled into the drive. An impeccably groomed, elderly woman, wearing fashionably sturdy heels and dress, got out. A younger woman, who I surmised might be a daughter or a niece, assisted her up the steps. I brushed off my T-shirt and dusty work jeans, then opened the door. Maybe they were Jehovah Witnesses. I could say thank you, but I'm already fixed in my faith, and then send them on their way.

The younger woman apologized for the intrusion, then nodded toward her companion. "This is my aunt. She grew up in this house. We were in the neighborhood, and if it's not too much trouble, she wondered if she could see it."

I grimaced as I thought of the pile of plaster on the floor, the gaping hole in the wall where we had just uncovered a sealed-over fireplace, the now-exposed rotten wood floors and the limp peels of wallpaper dangling from the wall I was stripping. How on earth could I shatter her childhood memories by showing her this? I told them we were renovating. She might not recognize it. It was a mess, really. They smiled, waited. I opened the door.

Perhaps it was the power of memories that cloaked the chaos before her in vignettes of childhood nostalgia. Her eyes sparkled as we moved from room to room. She pointed out where she had slept. There weren't bedrooms upstairs back then, she said, just an attic. The fireplaces went through both sides of the walls for heat. They'd had ornate mantles, but someone had stolen them after the fireplaces were sealed up while the house was being moved. The old family home used to sit up on the corner, she said, but when the family sold the land, her brother had it moved to this low spot near the stream. Maybe fifty years ago, she thought, which would account for the age discrepancy of the house we'd noticed in the tax records.

After completing the tour of the downstairs, her niece guided her back to the entryway. She paused. Looked back. For a moment we stood, each silent, caught in three time warps. She, I suspect, seeing what used to be. Me, seeing what I hoped would be. All of us looking at what, at this present moment, was neither.

The Lord doesn't let the metaphor escape me. I think of his words in Isaiah: "Behold, I am doing a new thing … Do you not perceive it?" (Isaiah 43:19 ESV).

I'm trying, Lord. By faith I believe. But from my vantage point, the situation isn't looking too good.

PART III

JACOB

Jacob is a scandal from the beginning. The powerful grace of God is a scandal. It upsets the way we organize life. — Walter Brueggemann

A MAN WITH A PLAN IN THE HANDS OF A GOD WHO HAS ONE TOO

THIS WAS MY DILEMMA: I knew God would never leave me. I knew he works everything for good, even the most doubtful of situations. I knew his purposes would be accomplished. I even knew his plans were not dependent on my understanding them, even though I frequently reminded him my name was the version of Marcia spelled with a CIA and, like the agency, I loved being informed.

Those facts reverberated on a spiritual level with me. But lining up what I knew with what I experienced was like trying to focus the two eyepieces of binoculars and then find the right branch with the bird on it before it flew away. I didn't know how to view the repercussions, not only of my decision to scrap our plan to buy a low-maintenance house and instead persuade my husband to buy a money pit with a gorgeous swimming pool, but also of our decision to start life anew in an unfamiliar place without any supports in place. We were so confident about whatever it was we thought we would gain that we hadn't counted on how much we would lose.

I didn't doubt the security of my spiritual state; it was

how things were going to work out in my physical one that scared me.

If I were suffering because of some noble stand of faith or some unforeseen tragedy, I would feel more confident in calling on the Lord for help. But I had no virtuous cause on which to pin my suffering like a badge of honor. Since our precarious plight was because of a poor decision—possibly a selfish, although not immoral one—I felt I needed to woman up. Accept responsibility for my actions. Take what I deserved. (Not to say Bob didn't have a say in all this, but I write from my perspective.)

Much of this was ingrained from my upbringing. I grew up in a working-class family in Vermont. Vermont soil runs thick through my blood—literally—I remember when I was five years old and ate some. One thing about Vermonters—next to their Green Mountains, guns, and maple syrup, they pride themselves on their spirit of independence and individualism. They tough it out. I can still picture my father's hand with a fishhook dangling from his thumb, as he gripped the steering wheel of our '50s-something car. We were way up in the mountains fishing a trout stream. Dad had spent an hour untangling one kid's line from a tree and replacing bait on another, when he drove a fishhook, way past the barb, into his finger. Mom didn't drive. Cell phones wouldn't be popular for another fifty years. Mountain towns didn't have walk-in clinics. You did whatever you had to do—in this case, drive around the mountains with a worried woman and car full of sniffling kids until you found the house with a sign out front identifying a doctor who would cut it out, bandage your thumb, and send you on your way.

By not sticking to our plan but veering off with one of my own, I had driven a barb into our dream. So did I have any right to hope for an undeserved divine bailout? Where did helping yourself end and dependence on God begin?

Night after night, I'd reach over and pat the empty spot on Bob's side of the bed. The indentation where he had been had long since cooled. I knew he'd be on the couch, trying to wrap himself in a mantle of praise to ward off the spirit of heaviness and gain a sliver of hope from the Lord. I tried the same from between my Egyptian cotton sheets.

One night a dream preceded what had by then become my usual 3:00 a.m. insomnia. In it, I was hiding with two children at the bottom of a dark stairway. A man was coming after us. After he walked past, we ran to the top of the stairs. I yelled to the kids, "Go, go, go," and then turned to face the looming, black-shrouded enemy coming up behind me. Just as he reached me, I turned and said, "Well hello there, Monster Man," and pushed him backward down the stairs.

The dream jolted me awake. The father of lies might be having a go at me in the light of construction dust, dwindling bank accounts, and loss of identity, but at least in that elusive realm beyond reason and rationale, I was acting like one triumphant woman.

During devotions one morning, I wrote a prayer in my journal addressed to God by his titles of Lord, my Savior, Redeemer, the Mighty One of Jacob. Wait—The Mighty One of Jacob? Known more for his bad reputation than heroic deeds, Jacob was an odd one for God to attach his name to. Talk about someone needing divine bailouts from his self-made predicaments.

I'm thankful God doesn't shine up his heroes, Photoshop their flaws, and delete their flagrant transgressions. Not one to shy away from calling things as they are, God lines the family wall with a legacy of flawed heroes, partly for our encouragement and partly to show he is God no matter how imperfect his heroes are. Still, in spite of their weaknesses, people like Moses, David, Abraham, and

Elijah had some mighty moments that set them apart. But hanging up there with the best of them is one who's been described as a scheming scoundrel, a cunning conniver, a man full of self-serving strategies. So why is Jacob there front and center in the line up? His story spans chapters twenty-five to thirty-six in Genesis. And more amazing—his name, referencing both the individual and nation—is mentioned more than three hundred times in the Bible.

None of the snapshots of Jacob's early life are very flattering. Before his chubby cheeks even see the light of day, he establishes a name for himself as the supplanter, or deceiver—one who takes the place of another—by hanging onto his elder twin's heel as they exit their mother's womb. Later Jacob talks this older brother, Esau, into trading him the birthright due the firstborn, which in those days included a double portion of inheritance and title as family head. And if that weren't enough, Jacob later warrants some serious sibling rivalry by deceiving his blind, elderly father into passing the precious and powerful blessing intended for Esau, onto Jacob himself instead. At least that's how it looks from a human perspective.

Apparently, God sees it differently—as some of us have noticed he often does.

Jacob hightails it out of town to escape the wrath of his brother and spends the night sleeping out in the open with nothing but a rock for a pillow. It is here in sleep, while the man who always has a plan is powerless, that God bursts through and speaks to Jacob. The Sunday school visual of this encounter usually depicts angels going up and down a ladder extended between heaven and earth. The implication—we are not left here on our own. There is no disconnect between heaven and earth, between God and his people. God is accessible.

In the dream, Jacob sees God standing above all this. And then God speaks. He promises to be with Jacob, to keep him, and to bring him back to the land that he is giving to him and his descendants. God promises presence and protection. And he promises to accomplish what he has deemed he will do—without needing any help from Jacob.

Rather than having anything to do with his own achievements, Jacob's story is beautiful simply because it provides a spectacular stage for God to display his grace and mercy. Time and time again, the Lord personally interrupts Jacob's schemes and stratagems, his subterfuges, and side trips. Jacob encounters God, makes altars, makes promises to return, receives promises. He works twenty years for wives and wealth. When the Lord reminds him it's time to get on the road and go back to the promised place, Jacob schemes to protect his own hide, even though the Lord had already promised he'd do it for him. Jacob makes tragic side trips, but God is not deterred. He blesses Jacob with promises of protection, of life-long covenant-keeping favor. And the part I like best—he sees that Jacob gets home in spite of himself.

Now this was an encouraging story for someone who had gotten herself into a predicament.

HE KNOWS MY FACE

THE MIGHTY ONE OF JACOB. It didn't occur to me until later how perfectly this title for God complemented another one that was special to me. At a few pivotal moments in my life—usually when it was heading in a different direction—the Lord has impressed specific names for himself on me. The first time was when I was a brand-new Christian, homeless, in a city thousands of miles from friends and relatives. I'd run out of places to stay, so the pastor of the church I'd started going to offered to let me stay in the church nursery for a few days. As happy as I was to now be in the family of God, I didn't much care to be living in the church building. Deciding it was time to have a heart-to-heart with the Lord, I got up early that first morning and sat on the couch.

"God, if you're God, you know I have no place to go and no way to get there even if I did. I'm going to sit on this couch until you give me some direction." Ah, the childlike faith of a new believer! I fully intended to sit there until the Lord told me what to do.

I sat. I waited. I listened. Since I hadn't been a Christian long enough to have read too far in my Bible, I had no idea that what I was going to see was actually Psalm 46:10. A banner, something like the advertisement ones you see trailing from planes along the beach shore, appeared in front of me, with the words: "Be still and know that I am God." My first reaction was to protest that I already knew that part and needed something more. But wave after wave of deeper understanding rolled over me. "Be still"—don't fret, worry, and despair. "And know"—absorb into every part of your being, not just your mind, "That I"—the one speaking with you, "Am God"—God, with whom all things are possible.

I Am.

Like a term of endearment that only those people special to you use and know, I treasured this simple two-word name as my personal revelation from the Lord. It contained universes of promise: I Am everything you need. I Am able to accomplish anything you can imagine. I Am well aware of your plight.

It's a good thing we have all eternity to get to know God because it took over thirty years and another housing crisis before I paid any attention to another of his titles revealed in the next verse of that same psalm. Although I'd probably read it hundreds of times, as I sat in the midst of the dust and debris of our renovation, it was as though I were seeing it for the first time—"The LORD of hosts is with [me], the God of Jacob is [my] stronghold" (Psalm 46:11). The Lord of hosts, the God of all, and every created thing is also the God of the one—Jacob. Me. It's easy to gloss over but staggering to contemplate.

One weekend we took a break from the renovation and visited one of our sons and his family in Maryland. I was walking back from the beach with my granddaughter who had just started kindergarten. Shelby was one of those old-beyond-her-years children who'd learned to compose herself in any situation.

But sometimes her face betrayed what she was thinking or feeling, whether pleasure or disdain, in the tiniest expressions. I asked about her friends at school. She said she liked one boy in particular. When I asked why, she said, "He knows my face."

He knows my face. Powerful words packed in simplicity. I'd marvel over them on those sleepless nights to come when I'd stand on the back deck and look at the stars above me. How mind-boggling it is that the One who created that vastness knows my face. He knows how I think and feel. He's not deterred by my wanderings and side trips, my flailing of faith and frailties. He also walked this earth, ate, slept, wept, and left a tangible image I can relate to. Glory in a brown tunic.

The LORD of hosts, the God of Jacob. He knows my face.

CAPTIVES IN THE JUNGLE

ONE OF THE most remarkable things in Jacob's story is the number of times the Lord appears to him. This should be an encouragement to those of us who still struggle with the idea of earning God's favor. Even if it were possible to do something to make God show himself, Jacob wasn't doing it. He didn't spend time in sackcloth and ashes seeking God's face, nonetheless, the Lord intersected his path half a dozen times. Jacob didn't deserve to hear God's voice, to see him in a dream, to wrestle with an angel of the Lord, to get a new name, to become the father of a nation, but God chose to do it anyway. His ways are unpredictable and certainly not dependent on our agendas or efforts. My experience confirms this truth. Much as I've tried to, I've never been able to make God follow my script.

But for the first few months of our move, when we were deep in the throes and woes of our blown-up dreams, I was so focused on my own situation, I probably wouldn't have recognized the Lord if he were standing right in front of me, which was part of the problem: a misplaced perspective. That's the trouble with trouble. Like a toddler throwing a tantrum in the candy aisle, it draws our attention—all our attention—to itself. It's difficult to stop kvetching and cultivate a spirit of thankfulness for what you do have when your myopic vision has its laser red dot zeroed in on what you don't. After all, I had a roof (and one that didn't need replacing at that) a refrigerator full of food, and a husband who hadn't caved under the weight of the constant construction demands of the past months.

Nevertheless, it took an awareness of someone else's problems to change my perspective and refocus me. I'd like to think this admirable inclination came from myself, but as it turned out, it was clearly a setup from the Lord, his gift to let me know he was indeed aware of our upturned lives regardless how they looked to us.

It started one December afternoon while we were enjoying a Sunday respite from construction chaos. Bob had removed the plastic dust cover from the couch and was watching a football game on the TV, balanced on a makeshift stand in the corner. I was reading the Sunday newspaper with an eye out for a part-time job. As I reached down to pick up one of the sections that lay scattered by my chair, an article captured my attention.

"Bob, listen to this." I held up a section of the paper and read the headline. "*Hostage: Here, we are living like the living dead.* The article says government forces in Columbia intercepted a proof-of-life letter from Ingrid Betancourt, a woman held hostage in the jungle for the past six years, along with several other people including three US military contractors. It's the first evidence anyone has had that indicates the hostages are still alive. In her letter to her mother, Betancourt describes living like an animal. She says she's lost her hair, appetite, strength and worst of all—hope."

I set the paper down and contemplated the conditions the hostages must be living under. To live as a captive in the degradation of a jungle camp conjured up horrors enough. But as resilient as the human spirit is, no matter how able it is to survive extreme heat, cold, blood-sucking leeches, and hairy-legged spiders, I couldn't imagine how anyone could live for long if they lost hope. My situation couldn't compare. It might be depressing to me at the moment, but it was worlds better than hers. Purposing to pray for the jungle captives and in the process, hopefully, to stir up my own spirit of thankfulness, I ripped out the article and stuck it in my Bible.

When the demons of darkness sat on my chest in the early hours of morning and skewered me with fears, I offered up thanks for my soft sheets and the roof over my head, as well as prayers for those trying to sleep in hammocks strung between trees in a bug-infested jungle. On December 6, my early morning journal entry read: *For those captives losing heart—To Him who is able to do exceedingly more than we ask or think—please give them hope, Lord. This day, break the power of the captors and set the captives free.*

Since we didn't watch much TV and bought the paper only on Sunday, I wondered how I would ever know what happened to them and when it was time to stop praying. Meanwhile, I decided to practice what I prayed and not give up my hope that we would still have enough money, energy, and sense of self left to forge a meaningful new life here after what was supposed to be a simple renovation.

One morning in July, six months after I had stuck the news clipping in my Bible, I sat at my new Silestone-covered kitchen island and booted up my computer. My home page opened just as a news flash banner scrolled across the top of my screen. I can testify that chills really do run down arms. Wide-eyed, I read the headlines: "Captives Freed." I ran to Bob in the other room. "The captives are freed. My captives are freed!"

Now, I'm quite sure God's freeing the captives was not dependent on my prayers. He does what he's going to do. Regardless. Nevertheless, not only had the Holy Spirit invited me to participate in what he was doing for some people I didn't know, but he also put the news on my computer at the exact right time for me to see the results.

It was such a quintessential Lord thing to do—seldom answer the pressing question directly but address the heart motive. I needed, wanted, assurance of God's presence in our plight. Most of my desperate prayers had focused on our own needs. Even though I didn't recognize his answers to my own present situation, by participating in someone else's need and witnessing God's response, I was able to rest in knowing he was well aware of mine. I felt like Jacob might have when he exclaimed after his first divine encounter, "Surely the LORD is in this place, and I did not know it" (Genesis 28:16).

PART IV

IDENTITY CRISIS

We are children of God, and it has not appeared as yet what we shall be. —1 John 3:2

HAROLD AT THE DOOR

FOR PEOPLE who didn't know anybody, we were getting an unexpected flurry of visitors. On yet another afternoon, the persistent ringing of the doorbell startled me. I looked out the window expecting to see a car but instead saw a bicycle propped on its stand. A slender man, in loose fitting, rumpled clothes and a smudgy baseball cap stood on the porch. Cautiously I opened the door, leaving the screened door closed between us. Without giving me a second to wave him away, he put up his hands, tipped his head sideways in a gesture of surrender, and launched into his plea.

"Please, could you spare me a few dollars? Something, anything."

Previously, the only encounters I'd had with someone's begging were on city streets where it was possible to toss a dollar or look the other way and walk on by. But right here, face-to-face on my porch? Not sure what to do, I hesitated, a nuance he noticed and pounced upon. Before I could say another word or close the door, he turned down his lips, furrowed his brows and put on the most convincing pleading-eyed pout I'd ever seen. "Please, Big Lady, anything you can spare."

Big Lady? I stood five feet three and fit a single-digit dress size. Before I could mull over this new moniker, I remembered how much money we'd spent dining out the night before. I believed if you didn't earn it, you shouldn't be given it, and I was reluctant to give money to someone whose hardship I suspected was a consequence of wrong living. But still, I didn't know this man's story. He looked so hopeless. I hesitated, then slipped a few bills through the crack in the door. He inspected them, gave a slight nod as if to say that would do, then peddled away.

His name was Harold. Every few weeks he'd show up on our doorstep, hoping for money but settling for a sandwich and drink if all else failed. Sometimes he'd bring us gifts—a porch furniture footstool or a dug-up clump of perennials, which I hoped he'd come by honestly. He called my husband "Big Dog" and continued to address me as "Big Lady," a title I later assumed meant he thought I held the purse strings of the household. One time when I wouldn't give him more money because I'd already given him some that week, he tried to wheedle some from Bob who had just pulled into the driveway. "Please Big Dog, just a few dollars. Big Lady won't give me any." Eventually Harold became such a routine part of our lives that he thought nothing of making himself at home. It wasn't unusual for us to come back and find him waiting for us on the porch—in the rocking chair. He'd get up, smile, wave, and then ask for money as expectantly as our kids used to. He even started telling me the ways he preferred his sandwiches and how he sure would like soda over water, if I had some.

As much as I didn't want to give Harold handouts, it was often more work for me to find something for him to do than it was to do it myself. I tried to save jobs for him like cutting the shrubs or weeding, but he didn't always show up on a regular schedule—or at least one I could count on. When he finally did come, he'd stand there with a fistful of weeds he'd quickly pulled from the flowerbed in the front and launch into his most apologetic tone.

"Please, Big Lady, I'll pull your weeds or cut the bushes. I know. I know I was just here last week, but I ain't got no place to stay unless I pay the woman. She rents rooms. It's eight dollars if I want a bath."

One time I refused to give Harold any money because he hadn't come back to finish trimming the hedges I'd already paid him for before it started raining. Harold put up a fuss, argued, pleaded, and then, after I shut the door, cussed me. He didn't realize my daughter, who was staying with us for a while, was on her treadmill around the corner of the wrap-around porch. She had formerly battled drug addiction and now had no tolerance for hustlers. She didn't like our giving Harold money or my letting him do odd jobs if I were the only one home. When she heard Harold cussing us out to himself, she jumped off her machine and lit into him all the way down the driveway. Harold didn't put a foot on our porch for the next two months. I began to worry. Although he was a nuisance at times, and I knew he gave us a lot of shtick, I didn't think Harold was capable of doing much more than he was— working his route for odd jobs and handouts. But return he did. Duly chastised, ready to accept whatever he got or negotiate a price for a job done.

Although I thought Harold was pretty harmless, Bob didn't think it was wise to give him access to our fenced-in backyard, so I usually let him trim only the shrubs in the front. But one fall we needed a major cleanup. Bob and I decided to hire Harold to help rake the backyard. It was a big project. When I told Harold how much I would pay him, he happily agreed. Knowing he'd work better if I worked alongside him, I grabbed two rakes. As we heaved leaves over the fence, Harold got caught up in the flush of feeling good about earning money. He philosophized how terrible it was that some people thought money grew on trees and just fell into their laps. "They should work for it," he said. And then, as if remembering his more common form of survival, qualified his statement with, "Or ask for it."

I had to laugh. Over the years my unlikely relationship with Harold would remind me that it's good to work, to earn what you want and need. But then there's this: There is something that can't be earned no matter what we do to "deserve" it. It's God's specialty.

It's called grace.

Flat out amazing grace.

THE PASTOR WITHOUT A PULPIT AND HIS DUMPSTER LADY

Meanwhile, it was time we started earning something ourselves. Signs of construction finally outnumbered those of destruction. The house was pleasantly livable, but it had consumed our designated savings. Most of the ceilings were Sheetrocked and painted. We tread on the new, rough subflooring as proudly as if it were a marble surface. We had arrived debt free. Now, a few months later, we were considering a visit to the loan department. The pressure was on us to look for jobs and start bringing in some income.

Bob has had two main jobs (not counting our six-month mission time in a Mayan village in Guatemala). The first as a union electrician in New York City, the last as a pastor of the church in Vermont. Although we were still a few years out from drawing Bob's union pension and needed to work, we weren't necessarily looking to start new careers. As long as we were involved in other meaningful activities, jobs wouldn't have to be the focus of our upcoming years. Nevertheless, when we left Vermont, we thought with our degrees and experiences we wouldn't have a problem finding something of interest to each of us.

Much to our dismay, online applications and resumes disappeared into cyberspace, never to be heard from again. All that confidence we'd had back north in who we were and what we could do was now as substantive as a shadow. We looked like poster people for an AARP unemployment article. It had been easy to say our identity was in Christ when we had jobs—Christian service ones at that—and money in the bank. Here, not only were we unemployed, we were unknown, or, as one well-meaning neighbor said when she went to introduce me at her neighborhood candle party but forgot my name, "This is the woman who moved in down the street. You know—the one with the dumpster in her yard."

The Dumpster Lady. I looked at the few remaining exposed wall studs and strands of electrical wires looped across beams stripped of their sheathing. Our house wasn't the only thing being renovated. Somewhere south of the Mason-Dixon Line, the box containing life as we'd known it had fallen off the truck, and all the prideful props that had subtly become a part of our own structures were now threatened. We were being stripped down to our own foundations. And the process wasn't pretty.

Bob, a man who'd had a title of respect and honor, was now donning the orange apron of the home building supply store whose aisles and products we now knew by heart. Not that it wasn't a respectable way to put food on the table, but it represented yet another stripping away of all things faithful and familiar. As he quickly discovered, there were no unions in South Carolina and that lower cost of living in the South came with a price: wages were significantly lower as well. Even his skills as a journeyman electrician brought in only a third of the income he'd made years earlier in New York.

When we'd told our congregation back in Vermont that Bob was leaving the pastorate, one man, a new

Christian who appreciated Bob for his down-to-earth, come-as-you-are explanations of Jesus, stopped by the house. "If you aren't Pastor Bob anymore, what should I call you?" Unable to bring himself to call Bob by his name without the attached title, he settled on calling him P.B. Although it didn't matter to Bob what anyone called him, we thought it was sweet of our friend to be concerned by the way to address the man he respected as his pastor but who was no longer. At the time, we didn't realize how deeply embedded our identities were in what we did, and that we too would soon wonder—what's a pastor without a pulpit?

Although I wasn't a certified teacher, all the jobs I had in the past several years involved teaching positions in the private sector. Since I hadn't heard back from some of the substitute teaching positions I'd applied for, I started looking at random ads for anything to help out.

I scanned the general employment column in the paper. "Hey Bob, here's one I wouldn't mind," I said. "It's for a security screener at the little airport not far from here." The airport was close, small, and manageable as far as airports go. An undemanding job appealed to me because we were still up to our necks in the never-ending renovation. I tried to imagine myself in a blue uniform with my photo in a lanyard strung around my neck, scanning luggage, and waving people through the security line. Not exactly how I had pictured my new life in the South, but how hard could it be? Hoping to beat the competition, I quickly scheduled an appointment for the test.

For a woman who can never find the baby in a sonogram, identifying dangerous items buried in x-rayed images of luggage was incomprehensible. The computer screen booted up. Images flashed by me. They reminded me of the scene from the old TV series *I Love Lucy* where the ditzy redhead gets a job putting wrappers on candy.

But she can't keep up with the rapidly moving conveyor belt, so she crams handfuls of the candies into her mouth.

As the timed screens appeared and disappeared in front of me, I guessed and clicked. Yes! No! I have no idea, so yes! and hoped something in the tangle of items in the picture of a carryon was indeed a knife. The test results almost beat me home. All I can say is that the country is a far safer place because I failed.

The next job attempt wasn't much better.

It didn't matter that I met the qualifications in the newspaper ad—no experience necessary, just a car. My anxieties competed with the rain for an excuse to turn around and go home. At Exit 34, I gave myself a pep talk: You can do this. You have a master's degree, a Bible degree, and years of teaching experience, to say nothing of all the traveling you've done. For crying out loud, you can deliver Yellowbooks.

At Exit 33, I flicked the blinker, swallowed the knot in my chest, and turned toward the warehouse. The rain slowed to a grey spit. I pulled into the muddy yard and drove around to the rear of the building where several vans were backed up to the loading dock. Synchronized teams of young men relayed armfuls of telephone books, stuffing them into plastic sleeves before tossing them into the empty cavern of their vans. I parked my car and got out to find the person in charge.

You would have thought I'd just kicked open the swinging doors of the Gunslinger Saloon. All eyes turned toward me, the only female in the place—a white, obviously middle-class female, wearing diamond earrings and a black leather jacket. While feeling as self-conscious as a kid at an eighth-grade dance, I nevertheless squared my shoulders, selected a route from the wall map, and backed my car up to the dock where the forklift was waiting to drop my pallet of books.

The sound of grating metal stopped me. Trying to look nonplussed about the dent I had just put in my Honda CRV, which I suspected was going to cost more money to repair than I would make in days of hanging directories on doorknobs, I stuffed my car with the yellow bundles and their plastic sleeves, then drove off in search of an empty parking lot where I could bag books and cry.

While some transcendent part of me appreciated the fact that God cares more about character building than situation, I wanted to arm-wrestle the Lord and, like Jacob, refuse to let go unless he blessed me, which in my limited vision meant change my circumstance. Ultimately, of course, I knew he was blessing me and would continue to do so. But I had no idea what that was going to look like, because more often than not, blessings don't come the way we expect they will. We're like the hungry Israelites in the wilderness when God provided bread from heaven. They called it manna, meaning "What is it?"

My Yellowbook delivering lasted three days, one of which I corralled my husband into helping me. Fortunately sometime later, someone rear-ended me, causing enough damage to include a repair to the dent I'd incurred backing into the loading dock.

PART V

NO LOOKING BACK

We made too many wrong mistakes. —*Yogi Berra*

THE VENDING MACHINE LADY

BEFORE WE CELEBRATED the end of our first year south, we made one more costly decision. It was as if we were following in Harry S. Truman's footsteps when he said, "Whenever I make a bum decision, I go out and make another one." One ill-advised move birthed five more. Like when you bite your cheek once, you bite it all day, or when you have a chip in your tooth you can't stop sticking your tongue in it.

This decision caused our remaining savings to shrink faster than Gideon's army.

In the biblical account from Judges chapter seven, God tells Gideon to lead an attack against the Midianites, one of Israel's enemies. Gideon is no warrior, but the fact he was accompanied with over thirty thousand men probably assuaged his fears of attacking the Midianites. However, the Lord puts a quick end to any potential illusions of self-won victory.

I imagine Gideon gasped, wide-eyed in alarm when the Lord tells him thirty-two thousand is too many men. After being asked who's afraid, twenty-two thousand turn back, leaving Gideon with ten thousand. Still too many the Lord says. Another test dwindles the number to a frightening low three hundred. Three hundred may not be enough for Gideon to feel like he has sufficient hands in the battle, but it's more than enough for the Lord to deliver on his promise of victory, which he does.

As for us—the Lord didn't have to reduce our resources; we were doing a fast-enough job of it ourselves. For people who didn't have a lot of moneymaking years ahead of them, the possibilities of recouping our losses and restocking the coffers looked slim. Without a doubt, if we ever went forward again it would be because of the Lord.

Still hoping for something easy to latch onto, we responded to another newspaper ad—one, which would have been better left alone. The sales rep scheduled an exceptionally prompt appointment, within a day or two of when we called. Said he'd come to our house.

On a pleasant summer evening, we sat in the gazebo by the pool and talked. His machines, new to the market, would fill a niche no one else had yet, he said. Just hire a site locator who'd find profitable places to put them, install your machines, fill them up, and collect your money. Yes sir, you could make a living doing this a few days a week. A mockingbird flitted across the yard; sunlight glittered on the pool. The prospect sounded like a perfect fit on a perfect evening.

We signed our names on the contract, handed over more tens of thousands of dollars than I care to admit, and became the eager owners of a half dozen combination snack/drink vending machines.

Since Bob was now working, we thought I could handle the vending business. Mondays I shopped for stock. Tuesdays I made my deliveries. The first stop was a lumberyard out in the boonies. The men liked Honey Buns and Mountain Dew. The next stop liked those too but requested a particular chocolate item that no one else cared for. That posed a problem for bulk buying. The third stop was an office in town—mostly women. They were fussier, requested crackers and diet sodas, which expired faster than they bought them.

The machine at the next stop was problematic. Sometimes, often, it wouldn't give back change. I'd examine the tubes of coins, find the jam, and spend ten or fifteen minutes with my little tool kit trying to free it up. At another stop I once found a note taped to the front of my machine listing all the reasons every item in it was horrible for your health. They had a point, but I hadn't yet found a package of vegetables that vended well. Besides, they were the ones who requested a machine in the first place.

After months of collecting small bagfuls of quarters, nickels, dimes, and one-dollar bills, I couldn't remember why we ever thought schlepping crates of cola and boxes of junk food at this stage of life was a good idea. It was hard on my body and we didn't make money. Plus, not being good with numbers made me a poor businesswoman —a fact the various tax departments frequently noticed. I'm sure there are many entrepreneurs out there making a satisfactory income with the vending machine business— but we weren't one of them.

My neighbor had introduced me as the Dumpster Lady. My bookstore friend called me Yellowbook after that ill-fated venture. Harold called me Big Lady, and now my chiropractor dubbed me the Chip Chick. For someone going through an identity crisis, I had an impressive list of aka's. If I collected any more, men in black suits and dark glasses would be showing up at my door asking questions.

I didn't mind delivering my chips to the blue-collar places where the laborers were mostly men, friendly and nonjudgmental. But I dreaded restocking the machine in the downtown office where, based on nothing except my own self-consciousness and pride, I imagined that the women in their silky shirts and black pencil skirts regarded me as though I were "lesser." Wouldn't they be surprised to know how many degrees I had, how many places I'd traveled to! Launching into my own Walter Mitty fantasy, I visualized how pleased I would feel if, while I was lining up the peanut butter crackers, as some of the women were sitting there in the break room eating the snacks they'd brought from home, I got a phone call from a publisher offering me a contract. I'd exclaim just loud enough for them to hear, "What? You want to buy my book!" And they'd look up in surprise because they'd dismissed me as the vending machine lady and didn't know who I really was, what I'd really done. Ah, the agonies we go through in our need to be seen by other people, to have them validate us. As if my worth were in my work, when I knew full well my real value was that I was seen and treasured by God.

The final straw came when within weeks of each other, one machine was damaged in a break-in and another needed a new condenser. We hauled them home to fix them. Like several-hundred-pound butlers ready to dispense soda, candy, and crackers to incoming guests, they stood on each side of the door in my now nicely renovated entryway.

One night we invited the pastor and his wife of the church we had started going to over for dinner. Here's something I've learned about Southerners: you may not know what they're thinking, but their manners are impeccable. No one blinked an eye or commented on the oddities in the hall.

I didn't want them to leave thinking I had some bizarre tastes in decorating, or I made my family pay for their snacks, so I finally explained the situation. The pastor's wife laughed and admitted she had wondered.

There was nothing "lesser" in being a vending machine

owner, but we knew this was not how we were supposed to be spending our time and talent. Even though it meant we'd lose our proverbial shirts, a few years after we'd bought the machines, we sold them, considered it a lesson learned, and never looked back.

WE NEED A NEW MAP

ONE MORNING A HOUSEGUEST, who'd come with a dog, told me when he reached into the dog food bag on the screened-in back porch, a large animal jumped out. Since it was predawn and still dark, he hadn't been able to see what kind of animal it was, but he spread his hands a foot apart to indicate the perceived size. I humored him with a surprised look, while in my mind I envisioned a mouse, or more generously, a squirrel. Certainly nothing as hefty as he was making it out to be. Nevertheless, I decided to give the back porch a good cleaning.

I worked my way down the length of the porch, swept behind the freezer, moved out cabinets of tools and other miscellany that normally would be in a garage, if we had one, but I didn't see any sign of mice or squirrels. A large tube of outdoor carpeting lay rolled up in the far corner. It was heavy, so I dragged it out on the deck where I could unroll it and check its condition.

Grasping the loose end, I gave it a flip and set the tube in motion, unfurling roll by roll across the deck. At the last turn, the rug flopped open and a startled opossum tumbled out. He sat up, stunned by what had just happened. In a second, his world was upended—one minute snug in an oblivious snooze, the next bewildered in blinding daylight with dogs barking and a woman screaming.

During the ensuing chaos of my corralling the dog, the creature managed to get his wits together. He let out a fierce hiss and then scuttled off to the safety of nearby trees.

Sometimes change takes us by surprise like that—an unforeseen upheaval suddenly shakes us out of our comfy rugs and alters the trajectory of our lives, for better or for worse. Other times change comes creeping so quietly we don't notice the subtle tilt in the axis of our lives until one day it dawns on us that our true north has shifted a few degrees and requires a whole different calibration. Like the snoozing opossum, initially Bob and I were stunned by how different the world we'd tumbled into was. Eventually we realized if we were going to embrace whatever the Lord had for us in this new time and place, we'd have to accept the new now for what it was and stop trying to find the church, the friendships, the ways of doing things that looked like those of the past. We needed to stop trying to find our way around South Carolina with our Vermont and New York maps.

PART VI

FINDING HOME

For everything there is a season, and a time for every matter under heaven —Ecclesiastes 3:1

IT'S SEASONAL

VERMONTERS JOKE they have four seasons—fall, winter, spring, and of course, summer, which came on a Wednesday one year. Well, maybe summers aren't that short, but anyone who's lived there knows that all too quickly those delicious sunlit days surrender to fall—that season when the sun bathes both northern and southern hemispheres in equal light, and the earth pauses as though in a sensuous stretch before tilting her north face away. Greens turn gold. Like the grand finale of a fireworks display, hillsides flaunt their flamboyant arrays of rust, red, and orange, then fade away as October light gives in to the gray that will cloak northern dwellers for the next five months.

When I was a kid, I marked the changing of the seasons by the food we ate. My father owned a small tree service business in Vermont, which meant he was able to work seven or eight months out of the year when the cutting, clearing, and spraying of trees wasn't held hostage to the weather. During the winter, Dad relied on his hunting skills to supplement the weekly IGA cereal, milk, and bread budget. The opening of duck season in October ushered in the non-prepackaged-meat months. My mother stoically plucked the feathers from the geese hanging upside-down on the back porch. November was as much about deer hunting as it was Thanksgiving. Although we kids bemoaned the death of a Bambi, each evening we would run to the window and watch for Dad's return from the day's hunt to see if an antlered head hung off the back of the truck. His motto was "if you shoot it, you eat it." On at least one occasion this kept me from picking off some squirrels, although my sister has since informed me that our winter diet did indeed include those arboreal rodents. In February, Lake Champlain offered up her bounty of little fish called smelt. I was thankful for two reasons: I liked smelt, and spring was in sight, which meant we'd start eating what to my child mind was "real" meat—the kind that came cellophane wrapped.

My mom had a row of colored glass bottles on the kitchen windowsill. She lined her window with the ambers, and indigos, and greens dug up from some abandoned homestead's dirt-covered dump. Colored bottles breaking the gray—the DIY home décor for women like my mom who dreamed about places in the books they bought for their children from the door-to-door salesmen. Women who captured beauty in glass jars on a windowsill like fireflies on a June night. Once my dad brought in a find from our own backyard. We peered at the sediment still trapped inside, wondered if it were just dirt or some tainted apothecary that we had better carefully dispose of before assigning a place on the sill. I suspect we just rinsed it out.

Looking back, my romanticized notion is that some weeks the only color you'd see on a winter's day was a glint of sunlight slanting through those bottles. But one day, maybe around the end of March, just when winter seemed too long, too cold, too tiring, and you couldn't stand anymore gray, you'd walk into the kitchen at just the right moment and see there on the windowsill, a shaft of light trapped inside a bottle of blue, blazing in a burst of prismatic glory.

Although Bob and I weren't seeing any blazes of prismatic glory in our own lives yet, we recognized the subtle hues that heralded a shift in our season of the stranger. It first manifested in little things—in the less-guarded edges of our attitudes concerning the world around us. In April, we peeled back the dense black netting that had covered the pool since we'd gotten here. I peered at the murky green water. A visit from the pool lady assured me that even though I couldn't see bottom on Monday, by Friday it would be sparkling clear. Everything in its time.

Over the next several years, the pool, that beguiling Siren that had lured me like an Odyssean sailor to this shore, would earn its keep. We were outdoor people and probably spent as much time in the backyard as inside the house. Bob ran electricity to the huge gazebo, strung lights around the perimeter of the roof, and installed a fan. It was there we wrote, we read, we entertained, and we began to ease into our new surroundings.

Bob started working with an electrical contractor and volunteering with a ministry for people with addictions. I found our family dentist right around the corner and my chiropractor at a booth at the annual Home and Garden Show. And I learned from a TV commercial that the place to go for fun for the whole family was the upcoming Gun and Knife Show. Gotta love the South. Although we never stopped being amazed that doctor offices, car-lube shops, restaurants, and stores boldly played Christian music, we adjusted to the language and lingo. We understood what the cashier meant when she asked if we needed a buggy and what the woman next to us in the elevator wanted when she told me to mash the button—please. Always please and thank you ma'am here.

My friend Valorie, who I met while working part-time at a college bookstore, has that broad, soft, sweet-as-tea Southern accent. During slow moments at the store, we'd huddle behind the bookshelves and she'd give me lessons in stretching my clipped, one-syllable i's into two. She'd say in her genteel Georgia peach drawl, "It's a *niice niight* for a *kniife fiight*," and make it sound as if we were taking an evening stroll. When I tried, it sounded like I was rallying my street gang.

On a whim, I signed up for a five-night writing workshop I saw advertised in the paper. Each week we were supposed to write something and share it in class. I wrote about my family's experience driving from New Jersey to Guatemala to work with widows and orphans in a Mayan village. After the last class, the instructor, Lyn, who happened to be the editor of a weekly news journal, turned to me. "Call me," she said.

Two simple words delivered in less time than it takes to sneeze. Isn't that the way opportunity often happens? You go through a long season of prayer and struggle with no apparent result and then in an unexpected minute, a breath of time, something happens—maybe a telephone call or a simple word spoken—and in an instant everything changes. For me, those two simple words from the editor opened the gates, and a horse I didn't even know I was sitting on suddenly took off.

With fear and trembling, I sat in her office. "I like the idea of what our town looks like through the eyes of a newcomer," she said. "I'm going to give you your own column." We called it "Finding Home." I thank God for people who are willing to let us make mistakes and grow into our own gifts. Although I had never written a published word and didn't even know what a columnist did, each week I wrote about what the town looked like through the eyes of a stranger trying to find her place—

about finding friends and finding church and reinventing life in a whole new place and time. The Lord was clearly going before me in what was to be the first in a series of providential events that would launch me onto a whole new journey. Over the weeks, readers responded to my columns. Some wrote to say how much they identified with their own moves here. One invited me to join her writers' group, another invited Bob and me to dinner.

Although we still felt like we were outsiders looking in, by the end of the first year, we had weathered a condition we hadn't even known existed: Relocation Stress Disorder. It's that sense of alienation, loneliness, despair, and disconnectedness that a great number of the forty-million people who move in the US each year, as well as many seniors who have to leave their homes, experience.

Like the seedy puffball of a dandelion, we touched down lightly, exploring churches, finding friends, and gathering a sense of place. And slowly, strand by strand, another gossamer thread of belonging anchored itself into the bedrock of that elusive place we sought to call home.

SHARING SPACE WITH SPIDERS AND
SNAKES

ALL THAT SOUTHERN sun was changing our attitudes as well as the color of our skin. One of the first clues that we were adjusting to our new surroundings came from—of all things—the wildlife, particularly the creepy crawling kind like black widow spiders and copperheads.

I suppose the North has its own share of dangerous flora and fauna, but familiarity is a complacent friend. Except for the occasional unnerving encounter with a bat in the house, or bear sharing the same back road blackberry bush, or a patch of poison ivy, there wasn't much to deter anyone from taking a hike in the woods or going barefoot around the yard. However, I was well aware the sultry, sunny South was home to other not-so-soothing *s* words like snakes and spiders, for which my old house with its damp, unkempt crawl space provided a cool sanctuary on a hot summer day.

When we first began ripping up the rotten hardwood floors, we discovered there was no subflooring—no barrier between the crawl space and us. No barrier between us and the huge hybrid cricket-spiders that crept up from the crawl space. These shrimp-like aliens don't need a pole to high vault themselves into the air. If you try to catch one, they'll launch themselves right at you. I nearly put an unplanned opening in my closet wall when one landed in my hair and set me thrashing. I suspected the house also hosted black widows and recluse spiders, but my biggest concern was that the cool, dank, darkness underneath my floors served as a happy hideaway for copperheads. My fears were not entirely unfounded. One service person had told us he had removed all kinds of things from the crawl space in years past—including copperheads.

Then one afternoon, just when I thought I was adjusting to our new surroundings and even dared walk barefoot around the pool, I came home from shopping and saw the termite service had left a note on the door: "No sign of termite activity. Saw large snake enter vent in crawl space." Understated as it was, the note got my attention. How large? What kind of snake? And what on earth were we supposed to do?

Briefly I considered sending in our daughter's fearless puppy to ferret it out. But I knew if anything happened to the dog my daughter would be unforgiving. Since I am approaching the age when my children will start having a say about my future, I needed to make sure their most recent memories of me were entirely favorable. I turned to that twenty-first century purveyor of information—Google. "How to catch a snake" generated pages of suggestions. Ruling out glue pads, egg traps, pronged sticks, and live mice attached to strings, I went to my defender and protector.

"Bob, what are we going to do?" I asked, knowing full well the answer did not include the plural we.

He knew it too. Although hunting snakes in a crawl space rated right up there with chasing bats out of a bedroom, he looked into the eyes of the woman he promised to love, honor, and cherish, squared his shoulders and said, "I'll go in."

He and the puppy, which slipped in anyway, entered the dark, cavernous space filled with serpentine shapes of wires, pipes, and ductwork. Eager to help, I stomped around upstairs in hopes of routing it out. Ten minutes later they emerged empty-handed. Bob closed the crawl-space door, leaving the fate of the snake for another day and leaving me with the disquieting possibility that I still had a houseguest. Eventually the initial flush of fear I felt at the prospect of encountering it waned away. Although I continued to scan the corners when I entered a room, I was ready to take on whatever animal life came with my new territory.

"Besides," I said to Bob, "I know what to do now if I find it in the house."

"What?" he asked.

"Throw a blanket over it."

He was curious. "And then what?"

I smiled. "Call you."

Actually Bob surprised me with how relaxed he was getting with all kinds of wildlife occupying our living space. I didn't know whether it was age or life at a slower pace that had brought out this deeper appreciation for natural wonders. Years earlier when we lived in an adobe house in Guatemala, he had no qualms about stomping the scorpions that crawled down our walls at night. Now, if I didn't keep my eye on him, he'd be sparing not only snakes but also black widow spiders—which he tried to do one Sunday afternoon.

One of our sons and his children had visited for the weekend, spending much of the time in the pool. After they left, Bob and I were enjoying a leisurely swim when I noticed something scurry away from what looked like a fishing line dangling down in the skimmer opening. Bob swam over to investigate. A spidery filament, one end attached to the edge of the concrete, the other, hanging just short of the water, was covered with bugs that were sucked into the skimmer. It was an ingenious trap. The fisherwoman waited nearby in a crevice between the concrete and pool wall. Not only did she sport her trademark red hourglass on her abdomen, but she also boasted a huge globular egg sack.

Bob marveled at her ingenuity. She had set up the perfect poolside access to her food supply. He was all for letting such a clever creature live there.

I marveled at her egg sack. She had the potential to birth hundreds of offspring. I wasn't going to share my hard-earned pool with a venomous arachnid. Maybe Bob wouldn't be as sympathetic if he knew she ate her mate. Wonders of nature duly noted, I convinced Bob to dispose of both kith and kin.

NO MATTER HOW MANY TIMES BOB
LOSES HIS IDENTITY, IT KEEPS
COMING BACK

I KNEW a woman who cheerfully told her husband he should be thankful when she frustrated him because she was his "grace-grower." That's one way to look at it, because as most couples discover, the marriage relationship provides abundant grace-growing opportunities for testing our willingness to love, honor, cherish, and forgive. Opposites may attract, but it takes commitment and confidence in each other, and in what the Lord is doing in each other's lives, to stay together when those differences aren't as endearing as they were initially.

When Bob and I met, he was a polyester-wearing, Jesus-praising, New Yorker who liked Yankees baseball and NY Rangers hockey. I was a cotton-only, newly saved, former mountain tepee dweller.

Back-to-the-land ex-hippie meets ex-party city guy. Two strong, unblended primary colors now wanting to do marriage God's way. We hadn't known each other long before we got married, but we naively thought just because we were Christians we'd be able to easily work out any differences and difficulties.

Having come to womanhood in the throes of the so-called women's liberation, I was unfamiliar with the terrain of a godly wife, but I was eager to learn. At that time the biblical culture we were involved in favored the traditional roles of men and women in divisions of labor. Bob was the head of household and primary breadwinner. I could work outside but was mostly responsible for hearth and home.

Within hours of our "I-dos," that ideal set off alarms in my newly-beloved's heart.

Driving back to NY from Montreal on our honeymoon, I asked Bob to stop in Vermont. I wanted to show him where I had lived in my pre-Jesus life, and pick up some things I had stored with friends.

I pointed to a dirt road that veered off from the pavement. "Turn here." A cloud of dust billowed around us as Bob slowed for a pothole. We passed a decrepit barn. "That's old Lehman's place. His cows were always getting in my garden. When someone commented on the moldy hay that he was feeding the cows, he'd tell them, 'Oh that's all right. I just turn off the lights and they don't know the difference.'"

The road narrowed. My Brooklyn born and bred husband frowned. "This isn't a road. It's a goat path." He looked at me uneasily as though his new bride had just stepped out of a scene from *Deliverance*. We collected my boxes and headed back to the highway. I was curious to see what I had considered precious possessions, worthy of storing, when I'd left that life behind two years before.

I ripped the seal off one of the boxes, reached in and pulled out my old nail apron, complete with hammer. Bob's face registered his surprise—or was it alarm. His wife came with a nail apron?

I didn't want my recently wed husband's manhood to feel threatened by my toolbox skills. When we got home, I ordered a book for him on how-to-fix anything, in case he didn't know.

After we'd been married a few weeks, the kitchen faucet developed a drip. Understanding that Bob was busy with work, I decided to fix it myself. I propped his unused how-to book on the counter, and after a bit of searching, I found the hidden screw that released the faucet handle. Suddenly a geyser of water hit the ceiling, shooting the inner screws and rings all over the kitchen. I clamped my hand over the gusher and yelled out the window to the neighbor. How had I missed the part about first turning off the main water?

That night, Bob took the pile of pieces and reassembled the faucet—without reading the book.

Now, after years of doing life together—renovating houses, living in a Mayan village, agreeing on churches, putting things back in the refrigerator on the right shelf, adjusting to whether the window is open or closed at night, or whether one should buy a house by herself—all those initial insecurities and differences concerning our roles have given way to an appreciation of each other's skills and gifts. Less threatened by our need to protect our own interests, we want to support God's vision for each other. Like water paints, the edges of those reds and blues of our individual lives have run together, making a third color—the color of marriage.

Early in our marriage, I was taken aback by the advice the pastor leading our women's Bible study gave us. He said to give our husbands room to make mistakes. I mulled that over and decided it scared me. My husband's mistakes affected both of us. But the pastor's advice taught me one of the best lessons on walking with the Lord I've ever had. Trust him. Trust the Lord with your life when life is unfair. Trust him with your life when you feel wronged. Trust him with your life when the familiar is foreign and you don't know what lies ahead. Trust him with your husband. (However, there was that bit of advice in 1 Peter 3:7 that on occasion I was happy to paraphrase for Bob: "Be nice to your wife or your prayers will be hindered.")

Another thing I've learned about marriage, at least our marriage, is that it is a lopsided affair. It doesn't always sort out in the tidy piles children make when trying to be fair: two red M&Ms for you, two red for me . . . one blue for you and one blue for me. Sometimes that fifty-fifty proposition we expect in marriage looks more like ninety-ten, when one partner's blessing requires another's sacrifice.

To all outward appearance, it seemed the Lord had opened his gift box and strewn opportunity and favor over everything I put my hand to. My weekly column had propelled me through a wormhole spilling me into a world of purpose and possibility in the Christian writing and publishing community I had never explored. I was happily following the yellow brick road to the place I felt I belonged.

But my traveling companion was not.

Bob was busy enough with his job and his once-a-week involvement with the addictions' ministry, but the flame that fueled his passion to share the Lord with defined direction spit and sputtered like a wet candlewick. It wasn't that he was looking to go back into full-time ministry, but finding his place in a town that had as many churches as it did street corners proved much harder than he'd expected. He involved himself in men's ministries, but soon discovered that as much as we didn't feel it, we were older than the leadership in several of the churches we were attracted to whose emphasis was rightly on children-driven ministries. Having been a pastor and teacher himself, Bob was perceptive of and frustrated by theological nuances and differences that went over my head. For the first time the church, which for years had been the focal point of our life, no longer seemed to fit.

Bob knew the Lord was doing some deep mining in his inner man. It was as if the surface of his life were being broken in order that all those truths he knew and preached, could become visible. I likened the process to the necessary plowing I'd read about when we were considering a trip to the volcanic diamond fields in Crater of Diamonds State Park. The ground has to be broken up periodically so the diamonds buried beneath can rise to the top, and all the hopeful seekers can find them. Nevertheless, it was painful to have that plow of God dig furrows across the surface of his life.

But one by one the diamonds appeared. Some in the form of peace and presence, some in the generosity of spirit to rejoice with me in my time of gain when his felt like loss, and some as humorous little reminders that no matter how often he lost his identity, it would keep coming back to him.

We pulled into the Home Depot lot and got out of the car.

"Oh, wait, I forgot my wallet." Bob stepped back, opened the driver's door, and reached into the side pocket.

I frowned. "You really shouldn't put it there." Bob grinned. He doesn't like to be encumbered by having anything in his pockets longer than necessary and will ditch his wallet and keys wherever he can at the first available opportunity. The problem is, he doesn't always remember where that was. One time we were in a major New York department store shopping for pants for him. As he discarded the ones he didn't want, I hung them back on the various circular racks stationed around the department. After numerous fittings, he finally chose a pair. But when we went to pay, he realized that he'd taken his wallet out of his own pants and put it in the first ones he tried on—ones that now looked like the hundreds of others hanging on displays in the huge room. Somebody was going to be happy to discover his pants came with a wallet if we didn't find it quick. It took a while, but we did.

Consequently, I was well aware my admonition to not put his wallet in the side pocket of his car now wouldn't change things. A few weeks later Jay, a young man who was trying to get his life together after doing some time in jail, started working for the same electrical contractor as Bob. Because Jay needed transportation to get to work, Bob gave him rides for a while. Then, since we were planning to buy another vehicle, Bob offered to sell Jay our car for far less than it was worth and even let him pay in installments. Jay was thrilled with the arrangement, so Bob turned over the paperwork and the car.

A few days later Jay called with a tale of woe. The car was gone. He said he'd parked it somewhere and it was stolen, but he couldn't report it because of complications with probation and licenses. And, since he didn't have a car, he wouldn't be able to make payments.

The people Jay was staying with sent us a scathing letter telling us if we pursued the matter, we weren't good Christians. Deciding it wasn't worth the fight, we counted it as yet another lesson in our southern saga. But then Bob remembered where he'd left his missing wallet—in the side pocket of the now missing car. Not only was he without a car and the money for it, he was also without a wallet and any identification.

Several months later we received a letter from an impound company in a nearby town saying if we didn't claim our car within a certain period, they would keep it. Our car? A quick call to the Department of Motor Vehicles confirmed that, as far as they were concerned, because

the title had never been transferred, nor had a new registration been issued, we were still the owners. Since we
hadn't ever received payment for it, we thought so too. But
what was it doing all those months to end up in an
impound lot in another town? I was leery about the whole
affair. Maybe it was all those police/crime dramas Bob
watched. What if the car had been involved in a crime and
the police were waiting for us to claim it? We had a friend
in law enforcement check into it before we showed up.

Assured the car was fine, no murders or warrants, we
drove out to get it. We peered through the chain link fence
of the yard. There it was, our little white Subaru, all in one
piece. Satisfied we were the rightful owners, the attendant
gave us the keys.

Bob looked at me with a gleam in his eye. "Let's see if
my wallet is still in the door."

I rolled my eyes. For crying out loud, the car had been
missing for months. It was found abandoned in a grocery
store parking lot. By the looks of all the trash inside, it
seemed as though someone had been living in it. But
eternal optimist that he is, Bob opened the door and slid
his hand into the pocket. Out came the wallet—complete
with a few dollar bills and all his identification—old identification he no longer needed because a new photo graced
the face of his license now. He turned and gave me what I
call his grin of grace—that triumphant look when once
again he's been bailed out of a predicament.

Regardless how cumbersome he feels carrying extra
baggage, Bob should wear a belt with a chain, because a
few years later he lost his wallet once again. This time he
had just come from the bank and happened to have several
hundred dollars in it. We were not only upset to lose all
that money but also to know that someone else was walking
around with our address and Bob's identity. Bob retraced
his steps. He called the bank. He called the store, but to no

avail. Once again he went through all the hoops to prove he was who he claimed to be and to get yet another photo on a license and a new set of miscellaneous cards with his ID.

Weeks later we received a notice from the local police department saying they had Bob's wallet. Someone had found it on the street and turned it in. There was no money in it, but his credit cards and identification were still there. The original finder must have thought he had the better deal by taking the money.

Clearly they didn't know the beauty of being Bob.

Not only was the Lord busy transforming him "from one degree of glory to another," but Bob had a collection of old IDs to show for it!

PART VII

WONDER

The world will never starve for want of wonders; but only for the want of wonder. —*G.K. Chesterton*

WHEN YOU HEAR THE SOUND OF
MARCHING IN MULBERRY TREES

BACK WHEN BOB was pastoring the church in Vermont, I led several mission trips to three different countries in Central America. On one of the trips to Costa Rica, the whole team bunked in various rooms in the same house. I woke in the early morning darkness and tried to slide down from my top-level bunk without waking Kathy on the bed below. But within minutes her pajama-clad form appeared at the door of the outdoor patio where I was sitting.

As we sipped coffee in the predawn quiet and tried to identify constellations in a hemisphere where north was south to us, to our amazement, a procession of ants—thousands, if not millions—each carrying a leafy green petal far bigger than its own body, paraded along the edge of the patio in front of us. Eventually the seemingly endless column disappeared into a hole in the ground. Not knowing the quick damage these leaf cutters do to crops—like strip a tree in a day—we delighted in having been there at that moment to witness such a marvel of nature.

Kathy got up to go inside and refill her coffee when she saw a shadow swoop across the room and fly down the hall toward the back bedrooms where the team was sleeping. I could imagine the chaos if people woke to an erratic Costa Rican bat flapping over their heads. Kathy is a forester by profession and an intrepid woman by nature. She got the broom and followed the bat to the office next to the men's bedroom where it had landed. Preparing to duck at any moment, I hovered in the distance, videotaping her as she opened the window and chased it out.

Later when the team gathered for devotions, we told them about the marvels we'd seen and showed them the video of how we had saved them from an unnerving experience they weren't aware was happening.

How often does God do the same for us—work miracles, fashion marvels and mysteries, and protect us from dangers that we, like the sleeping team, are oblivious to? I don't know if we'll get to see a video replay of our lives someday, but I have no doubt we'd be astounded if we saw all the times danger lurked at our right hand or wonders unfolded before us, yet in our busyness we were blind to God's presence or protection.

But sometimes we do get to witness moments of wonder. We happen to be at the right time and place on a moonlit morning as a silent army of leaf harvesters files by. Or no less marvelous but far more mysterious, we stumble into a moment when the window into things unseen opens and we get an unexpected glimpse into another realm.

I'm not one given to visions, but that's what happened to me one afternoon, as I was relaxing at my favorite summertime post by the pool.

The afternoon was so balmy even the flies were drowsy. I lingered in the last of the afternoon sun when a rumbling, rushing sound of wind caught my attention. Thinking a sudden storm was tunneling down the row of tall sweet gum trees that lined my property on the other side of the pool, I looked up expecting to see a darkening sky and blowing leaves. But the trees in front of me were dead still. Then, as the sound approached, the treetops started swaying, one after another, right down the line like an arboreal stadium wave.

Out of the wind, a column of tall people materialized, walking two by two. They strode purposefully toward the south—on top of the treetops! As they passed across from me, one turned to speak to her partner, putting me right in her line of sight. A jolt of fear lodged in my chest. Was I supposed to be seeing them? What would they do if they saw me? But either they couldn't see into my world or they didn't care if I saw them and continued on their way.

After they passed, the rumbling ceased. Stunned, I stared at the now-still trees. What was that? If it hadn't been for that physical flush of adrenaline in my chest, I would have doubted whether or not it actually happened. But as thrilling as the experience was, I had no understanding of why I had been privy to it or what it meant. It never occurred to me to search the Scriptures for an answer. Who writes about people walking in trees? Until or unless the Lord revealed it to me, I had to accept it for the mystery it was and be content to marvel at the glimpse I had into the world beyond my own.

Months later during my devotion time I came upon this passage: "And it shall be when you hear the sound of marching in the tops of the balsam trees, then you shall act promptly, for then the LORD will have gone out before you . . ." (2 Samuel 5:24).

What? I couldn't believe there was such a passage in light of what I'd experienced months earlier. David received the charge while he was in battle against the Philistines. He was to wait on the Lord until he heard the sound of marching in the trees, then he would know the

Lord had gone before him and it was time to act— to bestir himself—and attack the Philistines.

Some Bible versions translate balsam as mulberry trees. Whether they were balsam, mulberry, or my sweet gums didn't matter. The message of the sound of marching was clear. Wait on the Lord. Don't panic. Don't run to and fro hastily. Be on the alert, ready to respond and act because the Lord was going before you.

Although I wasn't sure what I was supposed to do with that, it was such a startling response to my vision, I was confident the Lord was assuring me he had gone before me. Whether it was for a general call to walk in faith or for a specific matter, I didn't know, but I prepared to watch and see when I was to "bestir" myself.

Often when I don't know what to do, I'm reminded of the imagery in Psalm 123. It refers to the eyes of a maid-servant as she watches the hand of her mistress for a signal when it's time to serve. Although I have never dined in the company of royalty, I envision Downton Abbey servants lined up along the wall of an elegant dining room. All it takes is a subtle flick of a finger from the master or mistress, which no one except the watching servant sees, for them to respond. For me, (except when I'm throwing darts at maps to find a place to move to) that response to the Lord's leading is usually something as simple as just doing the next thing my hand finds to do. Because one thing always leads to another. The key is to begin.

Encouraged by my newspaper column and growing involvement in writers' groups and conferences, I entered the manuscript I'd written in a national writing contest. Although I had no professional training in writing a book, I felt deep in my soul that this contest was for me, and that I had a good chance of winning.

But after I entered, an inexplicable fear settled over me. Surprisingly, it wasn't the fear of failure but of success. If I won, would I measure up to whatever expectations people had? People who write personal stories expose themselves. They have no fictional character to hide behind. What would readers think of me after hearing how I thought? And the people I wrote about? Even more—the ones I didn't? What would they think?

For weeks these insecurities crept across my mind, injecting paralyzing venom into any excitement I had of winning. Even the vision of people walking on top of trees couldn't draw me into the peace of God.

One morning I came on a Bible passage that said the sons of Ephraim "were archers equipped with bows, yet they turned back in the day of battle" (Psalm 78:9). It was as though one of their arrows flew off the page straight into my soul. I knew God was saying that I, too, was equipped. He had given me my bow and arrows in the form of a story and the ability to pen it. Whether the story won and was published or not was up to him. By turning back in the day of battle, the sons of Ephraim showed their lack of trust in the Lord. "They forgot His deeds, and His miracles that He had shown them" (Psalm 78:11). What was true of them was true of me—either I trusted him or I didn't. No turning back. I raised my arms, drew back the arrow in my imagined bow and shot it into the heart of that insecurity.

Some time later the sponsors of the contest sent me a letter: "Congratulations!"

The logo at the top of their correspondence—a silhouetted form of an archer with a drawn bow.

RECKONING THE REALITY OF PRESENCE

"SEEING IS BELIEVING," so the saying goes. If you can't see God how can you know him—how can you put your faith in something invisible? That's the question some of my friends have when it comes to God. That's the same question I had in mind when someone showed me a hair-raising video of the forty-story high glass swimming pool that juts out ten feet from the side of a Houston high-rise. With one step, a person can move from a solid floor they can see onto one they can't. Talk about a blind leap of faith! Although their brain and eyes are probably in a state of alarm over what is perceived as impossible, the stout-of-heart entrust themselves to an invisible barrier that keeps them and almost 300,000 pounds of water safely contained above the bustling traffic clearly visible hundreds of feet below.

As much as I enjoy pools and respect feats of engineering, I feel far more secure putting my faith in the invisible engineer of the universe and trusting him to hold me up even when situations point to the contrary.

In our walk by faith we don't usually get to see an accompaniment of angels following us around like the ones that kept showing up on Jacob's journey. But even though we don't see God, he's left us plenty of evidence of his presence through the world around us. Sometimes he makes himself known in ways as sure and solid as the glass floor of that pool through experiences of divine intervention. Other times through the witness of his Word.

On the day our daughter graduated from an out-of-state college, we visited her at an apartment she was temporarily staying in. The door to the apartment was a thick, heavy, wooden affair with a curved top and black iron trim. I told Bob it reminded me of a dungeon door, although later the owner proudly told us he thought of it as one to a castle. As we stood there knocking, I had no idea of the shock waiting for us on the other side when we discovered the terrible state of bondage our daughter was in. Already in a hyper condition, she blindsided us with the news she was hopelessly addicted to drugs. Thank God, she recognized she needed serious intervention. Since we lived in another state, we were unprepared to deal with this crisis at that moment and had to return home to make arrangements to come back for her and her belongings.

I was distraught as I sat in my chair at home and cried to the Lord for help. I opened my Bible, desperate for consolation. As I prayed, this is what I came to: "The exile will soon be set free and will not die in the dungeon, nor will his bread be lacking for I am the LORD your God" (Isaiah 51:14-15).

The dungeon! Because I had specifically used that image to describe the door, I knew the Lord was giving me a personal promise I could take straight to the heart. I clung to it with all my might. We were able to immediately return for her and make arrangements to get her started on the road to health and healing. It was tumultuous at times and took the better part of a decade, but God's word doesn't come back void. Today she is a beautiful, free, Holy Spirit-filled woman.

But even if we do have times when we experience God's presence in an undeniably personal way, it's easy to forget them if we don't record them somehow. Biblical characters noted and named the specific geographic places of God's interaction with them. Samuel set his pillar of stones and named it *Ebenezer: Thus far God has met me.* Hagar named her spot at the well the *Living One Who Sees Me.* Jacob woke from his dream of angels going up and down a ladder connecting heaven and earth with God standing above it. He named it *Bethel*—the house of God. These places served as reminders, not only of promise, protection, and provision but most importantly—of presence.

I think noting the times and places where God has assured us of his presence is a valuable spiritual discipline that helps us to develop an awareness—a sense of expectancy—of his very real presence. Like Moses, watching from his cleft in the rock, we can't always see God coming but we can see where he's been. There's wisdom to be gained through the rear-view mirror. God commands us to remember his deeds because we are a people prone to forget. In fact, *remember* is used more times in the Bible (versions differ) than the word *forgive*. Unfortunately we remember the negative, hurtful, and tragic more than we remember the good and positive. We remember the big events but overlook the minor moments. However it's often in those quiet, ordinary times that God is working.

Setting our Ebenezer stones of remembrance helps us to declare thus far the Lord has helped us and gives us confidence for the future. When I recorded different meaningful events of my life on a timeline, I was amazed at the people, places, and ways in my past the Lord used to intervene, whether I was aware of him or not. More than a few of my encounters with the Lord have been in hard places, stripping places, dangerous places. But a few years into our move south, the Lord met me at a new kind of place—a happy, expectant place. A place of new direction. I've marked the spot with a little stone pillar both in my mind and in my journal.

It was the second morning of the annual writers' conference, tucked away in the Blue Ridge Mountains of North Carolina. Hundreds of industry professionals—agents, editors, workshop presenters—and excited, hope-filled attendees converged on the campus. The thick fog, which had hovered low on the hills and shrouded the conference center since we'd arrived, reluctantly gave way to the shafts of sunlit brilliance that broke through the mist and flooded the mountainside. As a kid I had always imagined these radiant streams were coming straight from heaven. It was a thought worth giving in to as I luxuriated in the beauty surrounding our secluded accommodations. Since I had already secured appointments with the agents and editors I most wanted to meet, I decided to skip the morning session and hike to the prayer grotto in the woods.

I followed the gravel trail to a little clearing. A footbridge spanned the stream that rippled through the woodland sanctuary. Mesmerized by the sense of holiness of the place and aching to contain the beauty that surrounded me, I stood on the bridge and whispered, "Lord, if only you were physically right here to share this moment with me."

Immediately a thought startled me: If I were, what would be different?

I was taken aback. How *would* it be different? Wasn't faith the evidence, the real-life response to things unseen? The point was abundantly clear. If I truly believed Jesus was with me now, that he never leaves us nor forsakes us, why should the absence of his physical presence change how I acted or felt?

I stood there for a few minutes, listening to the gurgle of the stream, breathing the earthy forest scents. I remembered a book I had just finished in which the author challenges the reader to be alert to ways God could use her or him to be a miracle to someone else. The idea was to get yourself out of the way and let the Lord do what he wants through you. Since his presence seemed so palpable, I thought I'd give it a try right there on the bridge. "Lord, if there is anyone you want to speak to through me, have them come here to the grotto," I whispered.

I walked up to the chapel on the hill and waited a few minutes. What a silly thought that was. It was eleven o'clock in the morning. People had paid a lot to come to this conference. Everyone was at workshops right now getting their money's worth, to say nothing about the warning we were given to be on the lookout for bears in the woods. Deciding I'd pushed the situation with the Lord too far, I headed back to the bridge. A shadow crossed the path in front of me as a lone figure rounded the bend. By the distress on her face, I knew she was upset. Immediately I was afraid I wouldn't know what to say. But I knew if I wanted to be part of the prayer, I'd have to be willing to be part of the answer, especially when the Lord did exactly as I asked. I couldn't just say hi and flee on my way.

Trusting the reality of his presence, the wisdom of his words, and his ability to override any foolishness on my part, I opened my mouth and spoke with her. She shared why she was upset. We prayed together, hugged, and went on our separate way. A few years later, at the same conference, a young woman I didn't immediately recognize approached me. "I don't know if you remember me," she said. "You prayed for me in the woods."

Yes, Beth, I did indeed remember. I set a marker of reminder on that bridge that day. The reality of the presence of God.

The same year that I met the woman in the woods, I kept running into another woman at elevators. No matter where we were on campus, an elevator door would open and there one or the other of us would be. Lori and I called ourselves elevator friends. This was particularly fun because writers at conferences go around practicing their "elevator pitches." An elevator pitch is the succinct idea of your book that if you found yourself in an elevator with an editor, you could pitch to them in the time it takes to go from one floor to another.

A few years later, Lori and I were both invited to be on faculty. I was honored, excited, and scared silly to be teaching alongside the big guys in the industry. On the drive up that brilliant May day, I thought about Lori who was flying in from Rhode Island. I was driving up from South Carolina and had no idea when she was arriving, nor did I know which building on campus we'd each been assigned to. The memory of our elevator encounters of years past crossed my mind. Wouldn't it be funny if I ran into Lori at an elevator?

I arrived at noon, but since registration didn't open until three, the campus was still deserted. Anyone who was there early was at lunch in the dining hall. Told that my room was ready, I took the key and drove up the hill where the building I'd be staying in was. I unloaded my bags and entered the eerily empty lobby of the 120-room, hotel-style building. How could no one be around?

The large lobby divides the building into two wings. My room was in the east wing. I pushed the button for the elevator and waited as it dinged its way down.

The door parted open, revealing its lone occupant. We burst into laughter.

"God's just showing off," she said.

All week I tried to calculate the chances of that happening. If I'd left home two minutes later or had been held up by one more red light on the highway, or if Lori had been on a different flight or left her room to go to lunch thirty seconds earlier, we would have missed the moment our paths intersected. Impossible to deny—something this precise had to be contrived.

Besides being fun, the elevator meet-and-greet served as another Ebenezer marker for me that signified, "Thus far the Lord has met me." A reminder to pull out whenever I felt nervous or insecure during my upcoming week of teaching.

I know we walk by faith, not by sight. I know experiences come and go, often taking the lesson of their moment with them. I know Jesus doesn't have to do anything to warrant my trust, but I'm glad sometimes he chooses to step off the well-worn pages of my Bible and show up in woods and elevators.

We try hard to figure out what God is doing, what different situations mean; perhaps sometimes the Lord's reasons are as wondrously simple as my husband suggested when I told him how I met Lori at the elevator—again: "Maybe God's just enjoying the journey with you."

PART VIII

THE RECOVERY STROKE

The recovery stroke is the position of a wing in flight that "produces neither lift nor forward movement, but it must occur for the power stroke to propel the bird forward."—Grainger McKoy

BEAUTY FROM ASHES

THE STORY I'd written for the contest was a personal nonfiction one. But since I was neither famous nor infamous, according to industry professionals, if you're not a credentialed somebody those kinds of stories didn't have much chance of being picked up by a traditional publisher. Nevertheless, God had indeed gone before me. And even nobodies are somebodies in his eyes. After winning the contest, my book caught the attention of a major publisher and my dream of being a published author was coming true.

I was savoring the moment of having signed off on the final edits when the phone rang. It was my daughter, now a grown woman trying to get a previously broken life back together.

"I remember what happened," she said. "That day when I caught my hair wrap in the barbwire fence."

I froze, pen suspended midair. She was referring to something that had happened to her while we were on the mission field in Guatemala when she was ten. It was the story I had written about in the book I was holding in my hand. For years she had sealed the memory deep in her being, but recent counseling had cracked the chrysalis and slowly the memory emerged.

As she spoke, I remembered blurred bits of the afternoon back then when I couldn't find her. The kids at the home for widows and orphans where we worked told me she had gone down to the river with another little girl. When she came back, she didn't give any indication that anything was wrong except to say she'd caught her long hair wrap in a fence while she was running. Suspecting nothing other than disobedience, my first reaction was to scold her for going off without telling us.

A few years later, she began exhibiting behavioral signs indicative of earlier trauma, so we sought counseling, but the source of her behavior remained a mystery. Still, we didn't think to trace anything back to that day. Now, as a young woman who had returned to the Lord, she was remembering fragments of an experience that happened years earlier. Through recent counseling a full picture had emerged, and now she remembered the event that had traumatized her way back then down by the river. Apparently, she'd had time to process the impact of this before telling me. Her voice was calm, as though the unknown assailant that had burrowed long and deep in her soul now stood exposed, an impotent specter.

But I was shocked. I didn't know whether to cry or scream. A horde of conflicting thoughts flooded my mind. What kind of mother was I not to have noticed something had happened that day? How could I have missed that? Why didn't she tell us? How was it possible she didn't remember?

After the first wave of that storm subsided, I looked at the book I'd just finished editing. I held it in the air and shook it. Lord! Where were you? Here I am writing about how we were worried to take our daughter on that mission, but knowing you are faithful, we trusted you to protect her.

Now I find out you didn't! I dropped the book on my lap. Should I even go ahead with publication? The storm thundered on through my mind.

I had hoped if we were obedient to what God called us to do, he would protect those we loved from any negative consequences of our decisions. Although I felt emotionally betrayed, did this new information really change anything? Wasn't God faithful no matter what the circumstances looked like? And couldn't he make good come out of evil?

I remembered a trip we had taken to New Zealand when our daughter was a little girl. A pastor came up to her before service in a church we were visiting and prayed that she'd have a spirit like Esther. The spirit of Esther! Being the woman of faith I was, my first thought was alarm—Esther was an orphan! Years later, as our daughter grew into a physically stunning young woman, I interpreted the prophecy to mean that in the hands of God even beauty can be an instrument of his purpose and he would use hers.

I pictured the young woman on the other end of the phone call. Her outer beauty was undeniable. But her inner beauty had been trapped for so long in terrible, dark places, both as victim and as rebel. She had struggled with issues of self-image, with eating disorders, and drug addiction. For years I prayed Psalm 124:7 for her, that her "soul would escape as a bird out of the snare of the fowler." But even though it seemed at times nothing was happening, the Lord was forming his new creation. She was sensitive to others, funny, compassionate. Now that this memory was exposed, it lost its power, and one more strand that had tethered her to the snare was severed.

But God was not finished. He was then and still is faithful, in doing as well as being. I could see her past, her present, and her future fit into a perfect picture. "Someday

God is going turn these ashes into beauty—a beauty that helps other girls," I said.

Although she paused, her response was sure. She knew it too. "I know," she said. "I know."

I looked at the book in my hand. I could send it out after all; its testimony of God's faithfulness hadn't changed.

A few years later, I would stand transfixed before a twelve-foot high carved sculpture called the Recovery Stroke and think back on that afternoon. The sculpture was part of an exhibit by renowned artist, Grainger McKoy. McKoy carves birds, feather by feather, in painstaking detail. Some of his carvings are used as molds to cast intricate renderings in various metals like silver and bronze. He makes things as small as rings. He also carves things as big as the breath-taking, twelve-foot high basswood model wing before me. It wasn't just the mind-boggling precision of detail in each wing feather that captured my attention but also the description on the corresponding plaque.

It said this display was a model of the recovery stroke. According to the information, the recovery stroke is the position of a wing in flight that "produces neither lift nor forward movement, but it must occur for the power stroke to propel the bird forward." Although it is the weakest position, the one in which the bird is most vulnerable, in the eyes of artist Grainger McKoy it is the most graceful and beautiful.

The recovery stroke. I think of those times in our lives when we are suspended between what was and what will be. Times when life pauses or—depending on the situation—gets outright stuck. Times when we feel as though we've fallen into that four-hundred-year gap between the Old Testament and the New, when God went dark. Silent.

Yet in the eyes of our artist creator, that weakest position where we feel the most helpless, where we can do nothing in ourselves but cast our hope on him, is our recovery stroke—a position of beauty. Necessary for forward movement.

I could see it in my daughter—the grace of the recovery stroke. That vulnerable place where the breath of God raises one of his signature creations from a heap of ashes and sets them soaring on high.

.

PART IX

SACRED INTERUPTIONS

The great thing, if one can, is to stop regarding all the unpleasant things as interruptions of one's "own," or "real" life. The truth is of course that what one calls the interruptions are precisely one's real life —the life God is sending one day by day. —C.S. Lewis

NOT SO EMPTY NESTS

THIRTY FEET of split-level decking connected the house to the gazebo by the pool. It was an easy seasonal extension of our living space and we were fond of it. But we weren't the only ones.

I was thrilled one spring morning to hear the old familiar fishwife shrill, "Phoebe! Phoebe!" coming from the woods in back of the gazebo. Like birds flown off the pages of P.D. Eastman's *The Best Nest,* a pair of phoebes explored and examined every nook and cranny looking for the best spot to call home. Phoebes like to build nests in overhangs, and the high rafters of the open-walled gazebo fit their needs perfectly. At first we were delighted—how special to share our space up close with nature, to peek at the mama sitting on her eggs. I watched the pair of them from the kitchen window as they flitted around inside the high ceiling space of the gazebo as though it were their own private castle.

Apparently they thought it was, because they didn't want to share. Whenever we set ourselves up in the gazebo with our computers, books, or lunches—no matter how quiet and calm we were—the female would flee from her nest and circle the perimeter, all the while chirping and muttering "Phoebe! Phoebe!" at us invaders.

Subscribing to "the earth belongs to man," not the other way around, philosophy, we sat steady, hoping she'd see we weren't a threat and return to her nest. But inevitably visions of cooling eggs and distraught mamas would nag at our peace, disrupt our concentration, and cause us to retreat to the deck. For weeks, we felt like trespassers in our own gazebo. The worst part was her fastidious housekeeping. But the droppings she cleaned from her nest never quite cleared the railings of the gazebo. Finally I strung strands of fabric and belts from the fan and backs of chairs in hopes they'd look like snakes and discourage the annual takeover. Undeterred, every spring the phoebes arrived to stake their annual nesting claim on our rafters and put up with our intrusions.

But the gazebo wasn't the only place being taken over. No sooner had we finished the downstairs and settled into a routine of living without renovating, than our own nest started filling up again. In our case, occupants arrived from two directions. Our daughter came from one. She'd lived with us before, between life moves. The first time she'd come with a dog but left without it, and we added a pet to our household. This time she was back with another. I threatened to flatten her car tires if she even thought about leaving without him.

A previous house owner had framed and drywalled the two rooms and bath upstairs but had never installed permanent heat or air. Since we hadn't needed those rooms as primary living space, they weren't a priority. But now with a semi-permanent resident, we installed a ductless unit in the bigger room and daughter and puppy moved in. The little room remained a catch-all for both her and our overflow.

For a few months all was relatively uneventful in our

two-parent, one adult child, and two-doggie world. Bob decided to take advantage of the time to visit his elderly father in Florida. "Pa" (a curious moniker, I thought, for a Jewish man from New York who'd never lived in the country) was still living on his own. But not for long. The man who'd played tennis several times a week, right through his eighties, and had cared and provided for family all his life, now wanted to be taken care of. Of course he could come live with us we said.

While Bob was busy packing up Pa in Florida, I surveyed our situation. Where would we put him? Daughter and doggie were in the only livable space upstairs. Not expecting permanent houseguests, we'd turned the extra bedroom downstairs into an office. The only other available room downstairs was the master bed and bath—our master bed and bath. It was one thing to move from house to house but to move from room to room in our own house?

I stood in front of the selection of double-high, queen-size air mattresses in Target. Thinking my sacrifice would be short-lived, I figured we could sleep on it in the office, and during the day, I could stash it behind the bookcase. After all, Pa was ninety-one years old, and weighed in at a hundred and ten pounds. He was getting frailer and more forgetful by the day. I didn't expect him to be with us for long.

We moved the leather recliner and extra TV into our—now Pa's—room to make it homier for him. He was delighted with the setup. He not only had his own TV and recliner but bed and attached private bath as well. Home-cooked meals also agreed with him far more than canned soup. By month's end he'd gained nine pounds and had fattened up like a Perdue chicken.

Every night at the dinner table, he'd say to my

husband, "You know what your wife's doing to me?" Then he'd wait for Bob to say, "No, what?"

"She's keeping me alive!" he'd shout with a grin as wide as his bony little face could stretch. He got as much delight out of saying this for the fiftieth time as he had the first.

Although we were thrilled to see how much he was thriving under our care, we realized the temporary adjustments we had made to accommodate him might not be as temporary as I first thought. I could handle the inconvenience of giving up my bedroom on the main floor, and the rearrangement of furniture to make more direct walkways. But having to give up my own routines because I was tethered to a ninety-something-year-old—well, that didn't come easily. Especially when it affected my mornings. That's when I liked to write, prepare lessons, or do whatever I had to do. Intrusions got me a little ruffled.

One day, shortly after Pa arrived, I fixed his breakfast, set him up with a crossword, and sat at my desk to finish an article due the next day. A half hour later, I heard the shuffle of his slippers headed my way. He stood at the office doorway "Do we have any errands to do today?" I told him we'd go in a while. Pa shuffled back to the couch. But trying to concentrate on my own work when I knew he was sitting in the other room, waiting for the time to be up, worked out about as well as trying to ignore the agitated phoebes. I closed my computer and helped him get dressed for an outing. We went to the store and the bank. By that time Pa was ready to go home for lunch and a snooze.

The next day I got Pa settled with his crosswords and again sat at my desk to work. Within the hour I heard the scuff, scuff of his slippers heading my way. They stopped at the doorway, "So, do we have any errands to do today?"

I stared at the papers on my desk and waited for the swarm of annoyed responses in my head to settle. What I felt like saying was upended by the question I'd learned to ask myself when an interruption frustrated me or I when I was indecisive about a choice: *What is the most important?* I looked at Pa standing there happy and hopeful. We went to the post office. By the third day, when I heard the familiar, "So, do we have any errands to do today?" I resigned myself to the idea that Pa was a priority in my coveted morning time. But there are only so many errands a person has to do every morning. I couldn't keep going to the grocery store.

Since it never mattered to Pa what we did or where we went as long as we went out, one day, for lack of a better idea, I took him through a car wash. By the looks of the last car he'd owned, I suspected it'd been decades, if ever, since he'd done that, so I wasn't sure how he would react to being all suds up and slapped by the twirling blue dervishes that looked as though they were going to shear the roof off the car. That used to be a secret irrational fear of mine— that they would not only take my roof off but also my head. For years, I would drive all over town to find a self-wash rather than go through an automatic one. The first time I braved it, I slid down so my head barely reached above the dashboard until I reached the dry cycle. But Pa never flinched as the first soapy jet stream blasted his side window. I don't know what he was seeing in that world of his, but he just stared straight ahead sporting a grin bigger than a kid on a carnival ride.

Meanwhile, our daughter moved into her own place, freeing the upstairs. Once again we moved to another room in our own house. Although our sleeping arrangements were more comfortable, all those great and mighty things I'd thought I'd lay at the Lord's feet were looking more like daily oatmeal, a morning ride—not too long— companionship for crossword puzzles, and nightly *Wheel of Fortune* and *Jeopardy*. I reflected on words I had noted in my journal at one time by Helen Keller: "I long to accomplish a great and noble task, but it is my chief duty to accomplish humble tasks as though they were great and noble." And I hoped I could offer the Lord those insignificant tasks that tested my spiritual mettle before I'd murmured my reward away.

One day I started through the dining room but stopped in front of the Shaker cupboard. The door I always left open to display my special dishes and family mementos was closed. Again. I never saw Pa do it, but every day he closed it. Surely he knew I wanted it open— didn't he? I wondered if Pa were playing games with me, or if he closed the cupboard door every day as part of the routine and order he needed to function.

It was hard to know because so much of the time he was lucid, but then he would do things like stand in the middle of the room and wonder which way his bedroom was, or splat a spoonful of oatmeal on the floor for the dog who always sat at his feet at the breakfast counter because she knew it was coming. He did this when he thought I wasn't looking, but when I'd catch him and say, "Pa, don't do that," he'd act duly apologetic and promise, "I'll never do it again."

But he would. The very next morning. When I wasn't looking.

I sighed and opened the Shaker cupboard door. We were all trying to figure out these motions of grace and compassion and fitting someone else's life into our own.

A year after Pa moved in, I went to the kitchen and poured my coffee. There was no need to make oatmeal on this February morning. I walked into the dining room. The Shaker cabinet door lay open the way I liked it. I paused, then gently closed it. The place on the couch where Pa usually sat was empty. His crossword book folded to the last page he'd worked on. He'd given himself a score of 40 percent.

I sat at my desk and tried to write but nothing took shape. I missed the scuffling of slippers headed to my door, the daily "So, do we have any errands to do today?" The interruptions I once dreaded, now treasured memories.

I closed my computer and picked up my keys. Maybe I had some errands I could do after all.

PART X

A TIME TO BUILD: A TIME TO UNBUILD

[Along their journey to the king's palace] the carpenter still felt the need to build a home from time to time. The unbuilder made sure he understood what he was doing and then let him do it if he really wanted to. While the carpenter labored, the unbuilder, his guide and friend, would continue the silent waiting in the yard under a tree, and soon they would unbuild yet another house and begin the journey again.— from The Carpenter and the Unbuilder: *"The Invitation," by David M. Griebner*

WE DO IT AGAIN

HAD it not been for the early morning light shimmering off the strip of zig-zags in the middle of the humungous web stretched across a corner of my deck, I would have planted myself in the center of it. The architect of this translucent marvel, strung between a patio chair on one side and the grill on the other, waited nearby. She was a fierce beauty with her long pincer legs and rotund abdomen splashed with brilliant yellow and black etchings.

Argiope Aurantia, an orb weaver—relative of Aranea in Charlotte's Web—more commonly known as the writing spider. An old wives' tale warns if she spells your name, you're dead. I knew it was just a saying, but I took a closer look at the zigs and zags. From another angle they could be construed as MMMMMM—Marcia Moston.

The next morning, wise and wary, I stepped onto the deck, but everything was gone. Later I found Argiope hanging her new silks on the opposite corner. Apparently each night these spiders take their whole intricate webbing down, eat it, and start "writing" all over. All that precision, beauty, practicality, rolled up, erased, and rebuilt —each day.

. . .

Like my writing spider, I was ready to pack in my beautiful handiwork and move on. We had done all we could with this renovation. The Lord had dug deep into the foundation of our lives. I hoped he was ready to show us a new thing. And for me, that included a new place.

Some people are settlers. They can travel millions of miles on their spiritual journey without uprooting their physical lives a city block. My friend, Carol, lives on land that has been in her husband's family since the 1600s. She's surrounded by generations of relatives who live nearby. Their roots go as deep as the oak, pecan, and black walnut trees that cover their property. Her grown children tell her how much they appreciate the history their family has with the townspeople; it makes them feel loved and cared for, like they belong to something bigger than themselves.

Others of us are sojourners as much in the physical world as in the spiritual. We get new perspectives on our faith and purpose in unfamiliar places, places of transition and uncertainty. By some accounts, the average North American moves eleven times over the course of a lifetime. I've moved more than twice that. Like mile markers on the spiritual highway, my past dwelling places are representative of lessons I've learned in the hands of the Lord, whether I recognized his presence at the time or not.

As much as I admire, respect, and even miss the richness of life that being a settler brings, I've cast my lot with the sojourners. Settlers anchor us. Sojourners move us along. We need each other.

Although our house was now lovely, outfitted in tens of thousands of dollars in renovations from the roof to the basement and everything in between, it was still big and inefficient. With its turn-of-the-century charm and now modernized conveniences, the place looked great, but one thing was certain—no matter how good they look, hundred-year-olds only get older. And so would we.

Now that our nest was empty once again, we had more space than we needed. The towering sweet gums unloaded their sputnik-shaped prickly balls all over the lawn and pool year-round, making yard work a constant affair. And although light was part of my original criteria, I was so bedazzled when I first laid eyes on the pool that I'd been blind to how shady the property was. During the winter months when the sun was low in the sky, the dog and I vied with each other over the one patch of sunlight on the kitchen tiles. I did not want this to be my final house.

Every Sunday for several months we targeted areas on our map, drove up and down roads, tromped through woods and fields, looking for the perfect place or piece of land for our final home. I could go on Sunday house-hunting drives for months to come, but after our monthly searches stretched into years, Bob had had enough.

"We've got to decide whether we're staying here or moving." Bob eyed the side of the driveway. "If we don't make a decision soon, I'm building a garage, and this is where we'll stay." He was frustrated by all our talk of buying one more house—that small, efficient, low-maintenance one with a garage. That one I was supposed to buy years earlier. If we weren't keeping this house, he wanted to buy land and build. This time we could have some control, make it the way we wanted—and he was sure to get a garage.

Since he worked in the trades as an electrician, he was familiar with construction. One of his friends was a builder who Bob knew would work with us. But I was hesitant. We'd still have to do a lot of the work ourselves again. I'm the kind of person who walks into a house and imagines how I'd rearrange the walls. I can look at an old mess and see how to make it beautiful, but I wasn't comfortable with starting from bare land and having to put in water, sewer, and electricity. How much did all that cost? What if we ran out of money before we got the roof on?

Finally we put an offer on a couple of acres Bob liked. The property had beautiful mountain views, but it was long and narrow, much of its width occupied by a large mobile home. The mobile wasn't in bad enough shape to warrant tearing down, but I did not want to live in it. Being ignorant of the complications involved with moving a home that was registered with the Department of Motor Vehicles, we thought we could simply sell it or move it. Or, I proposed, we could cut it in half, live in the remaining section while building an addition—an idea our builder thought was certifiably crazy. Besides the impracticality of halving a trailer, we'd lose the equity of our addition by attaching to it. But Bob's heart was set on the land, and I didn't want to disappoint him. What to do? Unbeknownst to me, my reprieve was blowing in on a north wind.

Tenants had moved out of the mobile over the weekend and shut off the electricity. A sudden February freeze sent weekend temperatures plunging and frozen pipes bursting. For hours or maybe days, water gushed through the back wall and floors, unnoticed by anyone in the vacated trailer. Unfortunately for the owner, we had scheduled a building inspection for first thing Monday morning. A soggy, sodden mobile was grounds enough for us to withdraw our offer. I was relieved, but that was the last straw for Bob.

A few days later, when I went into the laundry area and saw him setting up to finish flooring under the washer and dryer (a project we'd put off years earlier) I knew there was no time to lose. He was either going to sell or settle. Now.

I logged on to a real estate site, printed out the most recent land listings, and with a quick, "See you later," headed out the door.

The listing said it was vacant. No mention of a building. I bounced up the long, rutted, gravel drive and stared at the mobile home entombed under a riotous mess of overgrown bushes. What was it with old trailers and me! Mildewed bamboo shades covered every window—on the outside. By their weathered appearance I knew they hadn't been lifted in years. I got out of the car and checked the listing again. That's what it said. Vacant.

Cautiously I ducked under the canopy of vines covering a small rotted porch. It reminded me of an unruly entrance to a Hobbit hole. I knocked anyway. Then tried the doorknob. To my surprise, the door creaked open, spilling a shaft of daylight into a dark cavern. My eyes adjusted to the blackness and swept across a living room, dining area, and hallway. Piles of papers, stacks of old telephone directories, unopened mail, clothes, and furniture covered every surface and inch of the floor. A lineup of TVs, in progressively decrepit condition, faced a sagging recliner. The first TV in line might have predated color. Apparently as one broke another was added next to it. A Budweiser can on the end table next to it looked as though someone had just set it down and stepped out for a moment.

"Hello?" I waited, one foot in and one foot out of the door. I don't know what I would have done if someone answered but, thankful no one did, I backed out and surveyed the surroundings. The property was a study in the Second Law of Thermodynamics—things left to themselves fall apart. I ran down my checklist of the important: It was private. On a hill. Open to east-south-west sunlight.

Utilities already on property. Check. Check. Check. Check. Bonus—it faced a small lake. And best of all—affordable.

But every square foot of the three-quarter-acre property was overgrown. Brambles, poison ivy and shoulder-high weeds made the backyard impassable. The mobile was old, rotting, leaking. There was no question about this one. It would have to go. There was no pool to beguile me, no quaint old house to fix up. No garage. But like a photo emerging from a chemical bath, a vision materialized. As I surveyed the chaos before me, I could see what it could be. And as bad as the property looked, I knew anything near a lake at that price would go fast.

Maybe Bob had forgotten he said he'd never let me pick out a house alone again. I called my realtor Valorie.

She met me there, immediately. Armed with a flash-light, we opened the door, hollered hello a few more times, then stepped inside the eerie darkness. We could see two bedrooms and a kitchen to the right of us. On the opposite side, a hall trailed off into the darkness of whatever lay beyond. Neither of us spoke as we crept along the corridor to a back bedroom. Valerie shone her light on the bed. We both froze. A colorful quilt covered a large mound in the middle of the bed. An animal, a body? We watched to see if it moved, then Valorie called out, "Is anyone here?"

"If something answers, you'd better move fast," I said, "because I'll mow you over."

Not waiting for a response, we bolted for the door.

I hurried home. Bob was still in the middle of his laundry room project. I waved the real estate listing in the air. "You need to see this." Recognizing the urgency in my voice, he put down his tools.

I tried to prepare him on the drive over. Needs a lot of work. Beyond being a fixer-upper, but didn't he want to build anyway. Bob's a good sport. He didn't flinch when we pulled into the drive. We ducked under the vines and once again knocked, then opened the door, and stepped inside. Despite several plastic laundry baskets lined with trashcan bags to catch leaks and windows stuffed with plastic grocery bags to stop drafts and rain, the place clearly had been lived in recently. I noticed some mid-century modern chairs under piles of telephones books. Did all this stuff of lives' past that filled rooms and rooms come with the place? What history would we unearth? Would we even want to look through it?

We stood in the yard, each silently trying to imagine living there. Reminiscent of our first move here years ago, I watched Bob's face carefully as he did a slow panoramic sweep of the property. We needed to be seeing the same thing this time around.

He and I are quintessential polar opposites in our approach to life. With the exception of politics, he goes left, I go right. The good news is, if you keep on a circular trajectory, you end up running into each other at a whole new point—the place you were both trying to get to.

"Well, let's put in an offer," he said.

Twenty-four hours later we were real estate rich. Several people had also put bids on the property the same day, but to our surprise, the seller accepted ours. We now owned a double-wide that needed to be demolished and a fixed-up fixer-upper that needed to be sold.

Selling any house can be a daunting task. Selling an old house is like pulling the lever on marbles in a pinball machine. The process lights up every nerve of anxiety, high hope, crushed hope, rejection, and insecurity in the human body. I had to remind myself that although stressful, it wasn't a death or divorce situation, and it certainly wasn't too difficult a matter for the Lord. After all, he's been in the real estate business for quite a while—moving a whole nation into their promised land in spite of their side trips, back-tracking, and wanderings.

A day after we put our house on the market, we had an offer. They were a young couple, first time buyers who initially wanted a new, easy maintenance house but were suddenly charmed by our big, old southern belle. I knew their realtor wasn't a fan of their decision as she handed over their best offer. I also knew we shouldn't have accepted an impetuously submitted contract that tied up our house on the first day, causing dozens of viewings to withdraw their appointments.

Sometimes first options aren't the best. Sometimes you have to trust yourself to wait.

But we didn't. We signed the offer anyway.

A week later the buyers, along with their realtor, and the building inspector arrived on our doorstep with the intensity of hounds on a hunt. They traipsed up to the attic. My husband hadn't gotten as far as his truck when they came fleeing out the door, the realtor yelling something about seeing daylight in the eaves and the poor way some roof rafters had been constructed way back then. They immediately withdrew their offer.

Putting the house back on the market after a failed, or in this case, terminated, inspection really intimidated me. I wore the ill-fated contract withdrawal like Hester Prynne's scarlet letter. Every future buyer would know it and wonder what was wrong. We'd already put so much into the house; how could we possibly do all that was needed to make it like a new house? I worried for days. And then I remembered. Jesus was a carpenter!

Surely he would know how to rectify the ailments of this old house. (The fact that he also created the universe didn't escape me, but somehow thinking of him as a carpenter brought the problem down to size.) There's a story in the Jewish *Book of Legends* of a woman who was building a house and discovered the beams were too short to reach the opposite wall. She went to the rabbi who prayed that her beams reach farther. Immediately they reached wall to wall.

I started praying to the Carpenter of Nazareth. Perhaps the problems weren't as bad as the previous people had thought. I asked him to send an inspector who understood and liked old houses.

We put the house back on the market. It quickly went under contract a second time and was again scheduled for an inspection. For the next week, anxiety stuck closer than my shadow on a sunny day. Morning, noon, and night I beseeched the Carpenter of Nazareth to fortify old beams in the foundation, fill in ancient insect trails, and find favor with the inspector.

The day of the dreaded inspection, I left early to avoid running into the inspector. To my chagrin, he was still there when I came home. He rounded the corner as I was hurrying to the door.

"Are you the homeowner?" he asked.

The jig was up. I hesitated, expecting the worse, then turned to face him. "I am."

"Great house," he said.

THE THINGS WE LEAVE BEHIND

ONCE AGAIN WE sold a house before we had another to move into. But what goes around comes around, and this time we were able to move in with our daughter who now had her own home. By all appearances, the former owner of the double-wide we now owned had been an ill recluse long before an out-of-state family member opened the door, walked him out, and left a life behind. Before we could do anything with the trailer, we wanted to sift through the artifacts of a family now gone. Bob was still hopeful maybe this time we'd find tucked-away treasure. The first order of business was the mysterious mound in the bed. As soon as we had keys in hand we headed straight to the back bedroom. Confident that the lump under covers hadn't moved from when we first saw it, Bob grabbed the corner of the quilt and whipped it back.

We added a pile of pillows to the dumpster.

I felt like a transgressor carting the history of a family to the dump, piece by piece: old skis, a sailboard, unused LL Bean gloves with mouse-turd-covered tags attached, clothes, bedding, dishes. Some things we kept or sold: amateur but good watercolor paintings, Japanese pottery, a mid-century telephone gossip bench, much like the one I remembered sitting at some time in my youth as I learned to noiselessly lift the phone and listen in to the neighbors on the party line.

In one of the soggy cardboard boxes stacked in a rusted shed, I found a decades'-old checklist of things somebody wanted to remember to pack for a ski trip to Utah: goggles, underwear, ski pants and ski socks . . . along with a sketch of a stick-figure skier sailing down a tree-covered mountain slope on a sunny day—evidence of a once happy, active life. Oh the stories contained in the objects we keep. Whether we make a concerted effort to leave some trace of our "Kilroy was here" or not, if only for a flicker of time, our moment is noticed in the things we leave behind.

My parents didn't leave much behind in terms of physical treasures, but they left a trove of memories that contribute to who I am. My father was a WWII vet, an infantryman who earned his Combat Infantry Badge in the Battle of the Bulge. He brought a lot of ghosts back with him from war. But we weren't aware of them. He never talked about the war, so we thought he was just an unpredictable man, sometimes generous and fun other times angry and sullen. He took a lot of solace in the outdoors.

I have one of his Ducks Unlimited prints and a cork decoy that, according to my brother, Dad carved from buoys taken off an old tugboat down at the shipyard. I admired his resourcefulness. He taught me to shoot a gun, gut a fish, and work hard. And get back up, no matter how many times I got knocked down.

The most important things I have from my mother are intangible. She could make a life-size igloo out of snow blocks and find the elusive jack-in-the-pulpit in the spring woods. She loved literature and read me long epic poems like "Sohrab and Rustum" even before I was old enough to understand them. She bought us all kinds of book sets the door-to-door salesmen peddled. I still have the first volume of *Journeys Through Bookland*, "A new and original plan for reading applied to the world's best literature for children," published in 1939.

My mother was faithful, both to my father and to God. Although I seldom remember her in the Catholic church we went to, I clearly remember her on her knees, praying for money to ward off bill collectors, praying for peace to calm a volatile husband, and probably praying for the ability to hold herself and her five-kid household together. She had a picture of Jesus on her bedroom wall. His eyes followed me wherever I moved, which at the time, I found both fascinating and creepy. Now I appreciate the fact they really do.

Research points to the importance an awareness of family stories plays in the emotional well-being and sense of identity in children, especially stories of overcoming adversity, perseverance, and faith. To quote Billy Graham: "The greatest legacy one can pass on to one's children and grandchildren is not money or other material things accumulated in one's life, but rather a legacy of character and faith."

I know many of us think if we shake the family tree a lot of nuts will fall out. Just a quick shake of mine came up with a Nova Scotia fur trader of dubious character who took up with a Micmac woman and was probably the source of the family claim to being part Indian. And a poor, landless family who made their living ferrying firewood and goods in their canal boat. Their reputation as thieves, however, earned them the title The Pirates of Lake Champlain. But they managed to make their name live on. A lawsuit they were involved in resulted in a case (Ploof vs.

Putnam) that is still studied in law schools today. I don't think these ancestors made any contribution to my faith, but they make for fun stories and do connect me to a history.

When the Israelites returned to the promised land after hundreds of years in Egypt, they found the wells, fields, burial caves, and stone altars their forefathers left behind—evidence all those years later that testified to the presence of their ancestors and their faith in the promises of the Almighty God.

That's what I hope my descendants find too.

DISMANTLING A TRAILER IS NO TIME-LAPSED YOUTUBE MATTER

To OUR AMAZEMENT, one of the people who'd also put in an offer on the lake land wanted the trailer even without the land. We were more than happy to give it to him, but as it turned out, the mobile wasn't so mobile after all. After weeks of trying to track down the title required to haul a home down the highway—titles that hadn't existed decades ago, but that the bureaucracy still wanted—the man abandoned his interest in it. So there we were with a big old double-wide parked right where we wanted to build. The person we hired to find the septic offered to bring his backhoe and knock it down for us. "$5,000—you pay dumpster fees."

Seems there's always a high price to pay to get rid of the old before you can begin the new.

Since we had already paid more than anticipated taking out the pine trees towering over our neighbor's house and clearing the land—including two trips to the ER for severe poison ivy (I'd been so proud to show Bob the shoulder-high pile of vines I'd cleared) we decided to dismantle it ourselves. After all—we were seasoned renovators. I turned to the Google guru of information and searched for "how to dismantle a mobile home."

Those time-lapsed YouTube videos make everything look quick and easy—stir, whisk, beat, bang and voila!—meals for a month, cakes modeled after the Eiffel Tower, dowdy rooms turned into showcases. Dustin's mobile home demolition video quickened the DIYer spirit in us. He made it look easy and for a lot less money. Bob and I watched him wipe that mobile from the face of the earth in five time-lapsed YouTube minutes. How hard could it be.

"We've got this," Bob said, overlooking the fact Dustin was probably twenty years younger than we were. Furthermore, his mobile's roof wasn't covered with layers of heavy shingle, nor was it sitting on a permanent, concreted cinder-block foundation.

One sunny spring morning, armed with sledgehammers, crowbars, and enthusiasm, we set off to knock out the interior walls. I understood why Chip Gaines of the TV show *Fixer Upper* gets so excited about Demo Day. Punching holes in walls, peeling strips of Sheetrock, prying up nails that shriek as they let go, not only releases a satisfying surge of energy, but delivers the immediate reward of visible change, of accomplishment, as spaces open up before your eyes.

Reality is no time-lapsed video though. Weight bearing or not, studs don't tumble like dominoes. For every five we knocked down, forty more stared back at us. Stud by stud, room by room. Inside walls. Outside walls. Windows. The dumpster quickly overflowed with rubble like a bowl of over-microwaved oatmeal.

Ceiling, toilets, sinks, and rusted shower stalls. Floor, roof, foundation. Weeks of tedious toil. Next to Bob, Perseverance and Endurance were my best friends.

Finally we were down to the last obstacle before we could start building. And that's when it kicked in—the peak-out point. I call it the Law of the Last. Why is it just when you don't have another driblet of energy, the last screw strips, the last paper jams the copier, the last mile twists uphill, the last swing of the hammer whacks your thumb.

We leaned against the truck and stared down the thirty-foot long rows of steel beams that we needed to cut before they could be hauled away. They might as well have been the hull of the Titanic for all the energy we had left. I couldn't stand the thought of continuing on but neither could we turn back.

And then came the gift—walking his dog up the drive-way. "Allen," he said, offering his hand. Allen was the neighbor down the street. His backyard was full of piles of scrap metal. "I have a saw to cut these. Happy to give you a hand."

And we were more than happy to let him. "Scrap the steel and keep whatever money you can get for them," Bob said. By the time we arrived the next morning, eight-foot lengths of steel projected from the back of Allen's trailer. Down the rows he went, slow and steady, sparks flying, saw screeching, steel beams disappearing.

A few days later we stood on the now pristine spot. It had taken us the better part of a month, not exactly time-lapsed speed, but like the tortoise, we'd crossed the finish line. With hearts of thanksgiving, we surveyed the site of our next home. No more patching old foundations and shoring up warped studs.

The writer of Ecclesiastes says there's a time to tear down and a time to build. We were more than happy to enter into a time to build.

Two of the three structures: the trailer, a metal shed, and a steel carport on the property were now gone. After we had cleared out the shed, one of the men with the tree-removal crew asked what we were going to do with the shed itself. It looked like rusted wreckage to me. I was astounded he saw any value in it, but told him if he wanted it, he was welcome to take it away. Early the next morning he arrived towing a little trailer. He spent the whole day steadily unbolting, unscrewing, and unhinging each section and stacking them on his trailer. By the end of the day, termites on a woodpile couldn't have done a cleaner job. Nothing remained but a few rickety pallets that had once held a floor.

Bob walked around the now vacant corner at the end of the driveway—nicely situated for a garage if he had one. Then he turned and pondered the carport, about twenty feet away. I could see it coming over him—that look. That faraway but focused gaze that meant he was seeing something I didn't see. I was seeing a large carport in a place I wish it weren't. Bob was seeing his coveted workshop back on the empty spot where the shed had been.

Looking around, he inventoried his resources: some semi-sound pallets, a crowbar, two small nylon ropes, a Toyota pickup, and a wife. Not much better than two loaves and five fish, but look at what happened with them.

Having previously sheared off the tops of the two-foot lengths of rebar anchoring the bottom of the carport to the ground and prying it loose, he tied the ropes to the back of the truck.

As he lifted a section of the carport with the crowbar, I shoved a pallet under the steel bar that ran the length on each side. Then I jumped in the truck and worked the clutch to inch the whole affair forward while Bob pushed the frame along the pallets. Like a game of leapfrog, every couple of feet we'd stop and reposition them, bring the back pallet forward to make a platform for the frame to slide over. Two feet at a time we worked toward the backyard.

If this were how the Egyptians hauled the rocks for the pyramids, they'd still be building them today. But with a lot of grunt and grind, we managed to drag that carport to the backyard and joggle it into place. I stood back to admire our labor. And that's when I got it too—Bob's vision. Instead of an old, ugly carport I could see Bob's barn. Although the concrete floor was yet to come, as were the barn-red sides I would paint, as far as we were concerned, the vision was firm as fact.

No more screened-in back porches. Bob would have his barn.

FOLLOW THE SUN

SINCE BOB IS WONDERFULLY agreeable to let me decide on matters involving the home front, I took on the research of house plans. Having learned from our last place how quickly a house project can consume a budget, we determined to make our wants fit both our needs and our pocketbook this time. Because this was supposed to be our last house, the one we'd live in until glory, we needed to consider every detail. I pored over a muddling magnitude of house designs. Ranches, capes, colonials, contemporaries. So many choices! Where to start?

My natural tendency is to over-complicate things, or as an expression I heard down here puts it, I "go around my elbow to get to my thumb." So once we settled on a one-story layout and got an estimate for the square footage we could afford, I asked myself the question that has clarified untold dilemmas in the past for me: *What is the most important?* The answer to that was light. I wanted our day activities to follow the path of the sun from sunrise to sunset. I sketched in the living areas and mapped the traffic flow. Reading area and writing nook on east side for sunrise, kitchen and dining area facing south side sun, den late afternoon, bedrooms on north side because they didn't need direct sunlight. Entryways and mudroom positioned so they didn't block important light.

I took my plans to my writing partner, Carol, who has a degree in house design. She took care of those pesky details like accounting for wall widths and making sure doors didn't open onto toilets, as well as suggesting architectural elements that added artistry and charm. Within days she had turned my idea into working blueprints. Bob's friend Kris arrived with his crew. Bob did the electric and I volunteered to do all the painting—a job I would later regret when I discovered it included caulking all the joints and seams in every window and door as well as all the nail holes. I was terrible at it. No matter how carefully I snipped the angle on the tip of the caulk tube, no matter how steadily I tried to draw a thin bead, the stuff would either ooze out in a skimpy line or gush in an erratic glob, which I'd end up smearing all over in an attempt to smooth it out. By the end of the day, gunky clumps of caulk caked my hands and clothes. One afternoon, the painter doing the exterior trim asked to borrow my caulk gun. I brought it outside and handed it to him. He looked at it as though I were handing him a fistful of swamp muck. "That's the nastiest gun I've ever seen," he said.

But the painting turned out well—except for the day I was on the top step of an eight-foot ladder staining the fence. All the workers were huddled under a nearby shade tree having lunch when my ladder rocked on its legs then canted sideways. I remember their faces—frozen in shock as they watched me pitch earthward. All I could think was to hold on to something, which in this case, was the can of stain, which splatted all over my face when I landed, still clutching it. One of the workers ran over and offered me his shirt to wipe my face with. All I could see through the streaks of cedar weatherproofing dripping off my glasses was the hem of a sweaty man's dirty T-shirt. And in spite of being stunned and not even knowing whether all my body parts were functioning, all I thought of his gracious offer was, "Ewww."

A few years later, after I stepped off a ladder a few steps too soon while power-washing the house and damaged those same previously injured ribs, one of my sisters admonished me that there were people who got paid to do these jobs. But that's the problem with DIYers—it's hard to pay someone for something you know you can do yourself.

Four months after we laid the foundation, we moved into our beautiful home. Everything was almost perfect— we had a lovely house and Bob had his workshop. All that was missing was the pool.

We had positioned the house toward the back of our three-quarter-acre property where the old trailer had been, because we wanted to take advantage of the utilities already in place. Most of our outdoor activities would take place in the smaller backyard, but I didn't anticipate any problem fitting in a pool. I knew where the septic tank was, and there was still plenty of room.

Still marveling that we had built a house and were going to put in a pool, I set up an appointment to have it laid out. Jerry arrived with a tape measure and can of marking spray paint. We marked out the legal limits from the property boundaries. I showed him where the septic tank was—we had already marked off its size.

"Where's the leach field?" he asked.

"Leach field?" How had I forgotten the leach field!

"It's probably right there," he said, pointing to the spot I had planned to put the pool. "You'll have to get someone out here to mark it off. It's going to be close." I suggested if worse came to worse we could put it in the huge front yard, to which he said, "Illegal to put it in front."

151

On the scale of world problems this was woefully irrelevant, but I worried. Shamelessly worried we had built our perfect little house but couldn't fit a pool. I hated to take such an insignificant thing to the Lord, but he knew what was in my heart anyway. So once again I prayed for a pool.

A few days later, a man with a ground penetrating radar machine and can of marking paint arrived. I trailed behind him as he wheeled his machine in back and forth patterns, stopping to squirt a line of paint dreadfully close to the last possible perimeter we needed. Finally he finished. I looked at the white marked grid and held my breath. I knew how much clearance we needed. Once he left I whipped out my tape measure.

I have no idea what our eternal living conditions will be like—I suspect pools aren't part of the architectural layout—but for now, with a few feet to spare, we were a go. I would have my pool.

PART XI

SECOND JOURNEYS

Second journeys begin when we know we cannot live the afternoon of life according to the morning program . . . [They] usually end quietly with a new wisdom and a coming to a true sense of self that releases great power. —Brennan Manning

THE BIG SMALL THINGS OF GOD

I'VE LEARNED some ridiculously random lessons in the school of life over the years. For instance:

- Depending on the sugar content, it takes anywhere from twenty to sixty gallons of sap and several hours of boiling to make one gallon of maple syrup. Don't do this in your kitchen if you have wallpaper. It'll steam the paper right off the wall.
- Down feathers can leak through the tiniest needle stitch holes. I learned this as a new bride trying to be thrifty by remaking a vest out of an old down jacket for my husband. Everywhere he went a little swirl of feathers followed him. He didn't want to hurt my feelings, but he finally confessed he felt like he was walking around in Pig Pen's dust cloud.
- No self-respecting daughter of a deer-hunting father should be caught hunting snipe with a paper bag and flashlight in the woods at night —or ever. I fell for this old trick decades ago

when I was the newcomer assigned to a VISTA project in northern Minnesota. I wanted to fit in with the seasoned volunteers who suggested, within an hour of picking me up at the airport, that I join them snipe hunting that night. They gave me a bag and a flashlight and told me to stand at the edge of the woods and blink my light. They'd drive the snipe to me, and I'd snag them in the bag. So I stood there in the dark blinking my light. Meanwhile, my friends had enlisted the local warden to play along and come "arrest" me for hunting snipe out of season—which he did.

Bible commentator Arthur Pink says God "suffers our dullness with wondrous forbearance." I'm pretty sure that's how my father felt when I told him about the snipe hunt.

Some things are simply one-time lessons, no need for review. Others are like fishing bobbins—they disappear under water for a while and then pop back up in another place. Often these insights seem so simple, you're sure you've mastered them—until they resurface sometime later and test you once again. For instance, one time we were vacationing on Captiva Island off Florida's Gulf Coast. Bob had had a busy workweek and was looking forward to doing nothing other than eating seafood and luxuriating in sun and sand. At six a.m. on the first morning, he opened his eyes as I was tiptoeing out the door. I had tried not to wake him, but he sat up. "Where are you going?"

I held out the shell-collecting bag in my hand. "Tide's out. This place is famous for its shells. I want to find a nautilus." I had seen a postcard in the tourist shop of a nautilus on a beach—its beautifully spiraled shell upright in the sand, waters lapping in the distance. Little did I know nautiluses don't come all polished up and neither do they live in the waters off Captiva Island. This Indo-Pacific beauty was a prop on a postcard.

Bob sighed. Got out of bed, into shorts, and with his own shell-collecting bag in hand, headed to the beach with me. It was a glorious morning. The cool hard-packed sand smooth under my feet, the salt air, sunrise-hued sky— everything a perfect seaside moment. But I had one thing in sight and one thing only—finding the nautilus. I hurried along, scattering sandpipers and gulls ahead of me. Occasionally a shell caught my eye, and I relegated it a spot in my keepers' bag. It didn't take me long to out-distance Bob who was making his way along the water's edge at a slow and concentrated pace, as if he were searching for a tiny gold coin from a Spanish shipwreck. He stopped often, examined a shell and either kept it or cast it. I could see his bag had a substantial sag to it, but I didn't know what he could be collecting that was so fascinating.

Later we met and shared our finds. Bob spilled out his —intact sea urchins, conchs, whelks, sand dollars, and numerous unidentified others. I had a pile of the unidentified others and no nautilus.

Bob had discovered innumerable tiny treasures that I— in my uninformed, single-sighted vision—had not even noticed in my haste to find the "big spectacular one"(which I ended up buying in a tourist shop).

The little things. Don't misjudge how big they are in the hands of God. He weighs that kind word spoken to a discouraged one as much as that fiery sermon delivered to a thousand. Not everything is a mountain-moving moment. Not all of us get to make speeches like the apostle Peter and bring three thousand into the kingdom—or even impact the lives of the kids in your Sunday school class in a spectacular way like the time Bob wanted to show them

God was as alive today as he was on the pages of their lesson.

Shortly after we were married, Bob and I team taught a Sunday school class in our church on Long Island. We were using the church's standard materials and kid-friendly Bible passages, but Bob was frustrated by the sense of disconnect the kids had between Bible stories of the past and their present lives. When he announced what we would be doing for the next week's lesson, the children in our class snapped to attention. So did I.

"Next week wear something you can walk to the beach in," Bob said to the now very attentive group. "We're going to watch Jesus calm the storm."

I smiled in surprise along with the kids, but my eyes bore into my husband with another message—*what on earth are you thinking?* Although he was an enthusiastic type of guy, Bob wasn't flippant about matters of faith. Whether it was divine inspiration or pure zeal didn't matter to me. I was flabbergasted that he had spoken so confidently in front of a group of impressionable children.

He wanted—in the case of this lesson—his students to know that the Jesus who calmed the storm thousands of years ago was still able to calm it today. And for some mysterious reason he felt confident it would happen the following Sunday, down at the little beach a block from our church.

Since this was in the days before cell phones and their handy seven-day weather forecast apps, I knew Bob had no idea what the weather was going to be the following Sunday. "Just how is Jesus going to calm the storm that we don't know is going to happen, and how are the kids going to be able to walk to the beach if it does?" the ever-practical me asked the ever-enthusiastic Bob.

Bob held firm with his conviction. "I don't know yet,"

he said. "But I feel certain God's going to show the kids how real He is."

That week we both spent time in prayer—Bob for his miracle, and me that God would bail Bob out of his predicament. On Saturday Bob disappeared into his workroom. A little while later he emerged with a tiny—maybe four or five inches long—hollowed out wooden boat. A few nondescript objects inside represented the disciples.

He held it up for me to admire. "Now all we need is a storm with enough wind to rock it but not sink it."

Sunday morning dawned bright and clear. Not a cloud in the sky. Not a breeze in the air.

I worried that Bob was going to look foolish and his lesson was going to be a flop. Worse yet—maybe it would only confirm the children's belief that God no longer worked miracles.

Undaunted, Bob brought his boat to class. The children were eager and ready. Since this was a small church where everyone knew each other, the parents apparently had no problem trusting Bob and me to take their kids down to the bay. They had swapped out their church clothes for beach-friendly wear. Bob reviewed the Bible story and prayed with the excited little group that Jesus would calm the storm and save the disciples.

Someone raised his hand and asked the question on everyone's mind. "How's he going to calm the sea if there isn't a storm, Mr. Bob?"

"I have no idea," he said. "But we'll soon see."

The kids chattered in animated anticipation as we walked the short distance from the church to the beach. Obediently they all clustered together on the slip of sand and stared out at water as calm and flat as a bowl of Jell-O. There wasn't a ripple or wave big enough to "accidentally" splash the toes of anyone trying to see how close they could get without getting wet.

Telling everyone to stay put, Bob took off his shoes, rolled up his pant legs, and waded out far enough to give his craft a chance to clear the shoreline and float around in the calm sea.

More than a dozen pair of eyes riveted on the boat as it bobbed on the gentle rise and fall of the tide. The miracle didn't look promising. And then, in an unceremonious moment, the little boat flopped over on its side.

Gasps of dismay, followed by silence, settled over our small band of hopefuls as we watched the impending demise of the disciples. But what else could logically have happened? I looked at the expectant, but now crestfallen faces, and realized that each of us had come to expect a miracle.

Suddenly, out of the vast blue sky, a seagull swooped down and scooped up the boat in its beak. We all whooped with *look at that* cheers and laughter, then watched in collective amazement as the seagull flew to the nearby dock and set the boat down. The gull poked at the boat, turning it this way and that. After determining its find was inedible, it flew off, leaving the disciples safe and sound on dry ground.

"He did it! He saved the disciples!" Everyone jumped up and down in glee and then ran to the dock. I don't know who was more excited, the kids or us. Bob looked at me. His grin said it all: "O' ye of little faith. If he can speak to a storm, he can send a seagull to save the day—and my hide too!"

All the way back to the church, the kids marveled over and over the disciples' rescue. They had no doubt the seagull was a divine messenger and that God is as aware of their lives today as he was in the lives of the men and women in their Sunday school stories of long ago.

. . .

Sometimes the Lord deposits those one-of-a-kind moments into our lives, but I think, more than not, we'll be surprised one day to see how much the little glass-of-water moments we thought were so insignificant ended up watering a field of fruit in someone else's life. All those "seemingly insignificant acts of daily life," as Andrew Murray says, are "the tests of eternity because they prove what spirit possesses us." They're the places where we have the greatest opportunity to either murmur and grouse or to act as though we believe our earthy lives, even the mundane parts, are made of the substance of the eternal. They're the places where we can prove being faithful in little leads to being faithful in much.

It was a lesson that would loom large in the southern season of our lives. We knew this was true, of course, but it was one thing *to know* it and another *to internalize it*—to not look at someone else's fervor and accomplishments and feel as though you're doing nothing except living your ordinary life in an ordinary way. To be able to understand and accept the shift that had imperceptibly moved us from being the center-stage doers to the backstage givers and supporters. I like knowing I've done some kingdom-worthy work, and I worry about that day when our works will be revealed by fire. Will mine light up the southern sky as they go up in flames? Or worse—sizzle and spit like a Fourth of July sparkler.

At times Bob felt that God had set him aside, "unstrung his bow," as Job lamented, because the fruit of his work didn't look the same as it used to. It lacked the definition and boundaries that a job or ministry provides. The Lord didn't seem as ready to respond in God-size ways to Bob's declarations of faith as he had in times past. And yet people came to him, one by one, for prayer, for wisdom, for encouragement—the young man Bob mentored who looked to him as a father figure and wanted him to meet his girlfriend before he married her. The friend in another state who called on his deathbed to ask Bob to come do his service. The daughter who looks to him for her questions of faith and life, who can't wait to share her funny stories, her problems, and her joys with him. The ex-addicts Bob occasionally gets to teach and encourage.

Sometimes I've felt indulgent about my determination to have a pool, but even that has been a means of blessing with summertime Sunday afternoon gatherings for food, fellowship, and sun. It's like living on an ancient trade route. More people have come to visit than we ever had in our other homes when we were busy with lots of coming and going ourselves.

One summer, missionary friends who were just beginning a much-needed furlough stayed with us for a weekend. For decades, they'd been managing homes for children 24/7 in two Central America countries. As Dena and I sat by the pool catching up on the past several years since we'd last been together, I told how I'd come to appreciate beauty as an attribute and gift of God. And that it was important to take time for beauty for ourselves and as an act of praise.

The next morning I went into the kitchen thinking I'd get the coffee on while everyone was still in bed. A movement outside the patio doors caught my attention. There was Dena enjoying a solitary swim in the early morning sunlight. A few weeks later she wrote to me from her in-laws' farm in Minnesota. She told me how important the reminder to take time for beauty had been for her, and how it had freed her to slow down and absorb the gift of friends, family, and fellowship with the Lord, as well as be refreshed herself.

All these tiny treasures from the sea instead of a prop on a postcard.

THE POWER-LIFTING PRESENT

THE FIRST YEAR we were married, Bob gave me some sort of kitchen appliance for Christmas. At the time I didn't appreciate household tools as Christmas presents and tactfully tried to tell him. I have since changed. A few years ago he gave me a pole chainsaw, which I was thrilled to get. This year he gave me some sessions with a personal trainer at the gym. Although I enjoy physical work, I'd rather haul bricks than spend thirty monotonous minutes on a treadmill, consequently I was delighted to have someone who could teach me specific exercises and whip me into doing them. I decided to observe the different trainers to see which one would be the best fit.

My sneakers made a gentle slap, slap as I plodded along the treadmill, logging off calories in tenth-of-a-mile increments—in contrast to the pony-tailed enthusiast next to me who pounded them off in mile clips. From my vantage point, I could see the whole gym. Trainers were busy with a wide array of clients, ranging from a man with a walker to another who looked like Bruce Willis on steroids. I didn't want to bore my trainer with my lack of stamina but neither did I want to be treated as though I had just gotten out of physical rehab. I also didn't know whether I'd feel self-conscious with a male, but there was one who seemed kind and helped people if he saw they had no idea how to work a machine. Maybe him.

Over in the weight-lifting area, a tatted-up, blue-Mohawked trainer was racking barbells. She looked tough. Definitely not a good fit. I eliminated her immediately. For the next few days, I wafted and wavered over which one to choose. I'd made decisions to buy houses faster than I was making this one. Finally, I decided to go to the training desk and choose somebody—anybody. Another woman had told me Traci, with the blue Mohawk, was good, but I was still leaning toward John. Just as the desk person asked me who I wanted, Traci walked by. "Her," I said.

At our first session, I told her I'd like to know how to use the machines, maybe tone my core.

"Let's see what you can do," she said, walking past all the areas with the machines people my age were using, straight into the most intimidating section of the whole gym—the weight-lifting one. She pointed to a formidable looking contraption and told me to sit on the seat, which was an inch off the floor, then raise my legs and plant my feet on a huge metal plate at a forty-five-degree angle above me. If it came crashing down, I'd be laid out flatter than a yoga mat. "Don't worry," she said. "The safety stop won't let it go that far. Now push."

Thirty leg presses later, we moved on to the second machine. I already liked her direct style and felt comfortable asking what was up with the blue Mohawk. "I've had four different kinds of cancer. After the first chemo, my hair came in pure white and in patches. I decided why not have some fun and shaved it off. I use a color shampoo because the dye isn't permanent." I was floored. So much for my making choices based on appearances.

During our grueling Traci-upper-body second session,

I learned she'd left the military for health reasons, suffered depression, and became an alcoholic, weighing in at three hundred pounds. It was do or die. She chose do. Joined a gym, quit alcohol, lost weight, and fell in love with power lifting. She now tries to help at least one person in a special way each day. I was glad it was my turn.

I told Traci's story to my husband and sister who was staying with us. My sister has an evangelistic spirit and can get a stranger in the Walmart chip aisle to let her pray for them. "Does she know the Lord?" she said. Bold evangelism isn't my strength. I felt a little guilty I hadn't been comfortable having that conversation with Traci yet, but I trusted the right opportunity would come.

On our third session, with a tension band around my legs, I did a squat-walk to the water fountain across the room. Traci asked if I minded drinking from a fountain. I told her after living in an isolated village in Guatemala without drinkable water, a fountain wasn't a problem. "My church is going on a mission to Guatemala," she said. And there it was. The opening. I squat-walked right back into a conversation with her about the One from whom she gets her power.

Two days later, even though I could barely walk down the stairs, I was still elated from my unexpected connection with someone I had initially considered not to be a good fit based on appearances. To my surprise, I chose to re-up my sessions just to spend time with her.

Even though it's been a recurring theme for me since we moved here, I've been slow to learn that sometimes the most delightful gifts come wrapped in the most unlikely packages. That what's best for us isn't always what it looks like at the time. More often it's the unrecognized gift of an unfamiliar place—the place where people, expressions, churches, and customs are different from what you've been familiarly comfortable with. But God's a patient teacher, and I'm learning not to look back, compare, or expect how life always used to be. Not to discount the different or hold on to the familiar way.

Often well-intentioned Christians (including me) have a way of tossing around abstract ideas as if absorbing concepts like "trust the Lord," or "leave it to God" were as easy as fluffing pillows. The bottom-line truth is—they are. But we're afraid to let go and "just do it."

My daughter has a miniature, black and white Pomeranian, appropriately named Capone. With marble-size black eyes and a little pink tongue hanging out from the space of a missing tooth, his face would melt a dogcatcher's heart. But if you get between Capone and food, he makes gremlins look like teddy bears.

One morning on a walk in the park, Capone snatched up a piece of cast-off chicken. Because he can't walk and eat at the same time, he clenched it in his mouth and dared me to touch it. I knew he wouldn't be able to bite me if I picked him up with his mouth full, but he would probably throw a hissy fit and drop the meat. Capone had a dilemma because he knew it too. He growled and tried to scare me off without opening his mouth, but when I grabbed him, he threw a full-blown tantrum. The chicken fell out—bone and all. Capone muttered and sputtered a while and then gave in and continued his walk.

Like Capone, we clench at things we want, or can control, or are familiar with. We want what we can see with our myopic vision. However, God's sees the long view. He sees the bone in the chicken, the soft heart behind hard tattoo. His way is full of hidden plots, miraculous reversals, and unexpected happenings. I can take great comfort in knowing he can call into being things that are not when I can't see any way to go.

Just before I met Bob, I was in desperate straits—newly saved, no job, sleeping on my sister's couch while I tried to put my life together. I decided I couldn't make it on Long Island and would head out, maybe go back to Vermont. But the pastor offered me an opportunity to stay a few days at a retreat center the church owned, where I could have a time to pray and fast. While reading in the book of Jeremiah, I came on this passage: "How long will you go here and there, O faithless daughter? For the LORD has created a new thing in the earth—A woman will encompass a man" (Jeremiah 31: 22).

That got my attention. I went back to Long Island, looked for a job and, better yet, found a husband. Within the year we were married.

Now, all these decades later, here we are in South Carolina, via New York, New Jersey, Guatemala, and Vermont. We have a light-filled house where once was a brush-shrouded cave. We have friends and family who often visit. Our church isn't (and probably never will be) the same in terms of relationships as the one we left in Vermont, but it is good and right for our now. Even with more years and adventures behind us than ahead, I can set another Ebenezer stone for whatever the future brings: *Thus far God has met us.*

HOMECOMING

Home. When Dorothy clicked those ruby-red slippers together and declared there was no place like it, she had Auntie Em and the homestead back in Kansas in mind. But for lots of people in our mobile society, home is a hard place to pinpoint. Is it where you grew up? Where you live now? When people ask me where I'm from, I say I live in South Carolina, but I'm from Vermont. Or is home, as my friend Felicia remembers, where your heart is?

She calls herself an army brat. She's lived in so many places that she doesn't know which one to claim as home. But during her impressionable coming-of-age early teen years, she lived in Arizona. Now as a grown woman living in North Carolina, she says, "Whenever I travel to the desert southwest, it feels like home. Nothing resonates as 'home' like the desert in bloom."

Early in my writing career, I led a writing workshop at a women's retreat. My class followed a marriage seminar held in the same room. It must have been an emotional workshop because boxes of tissues were stationed around the room. Thinking no one would be crying in my short writing class, I collected the boxes and stacked them on a table in the front.

Wanting the first exercise to be something everyone could relate to, I told the group to write nonstop for a few minutes about home. Heads bowed over paper pads; pens flew across the lines. I was impressed the topic had generated such a ready response. After a few minutes, I called time and asked them to share what they had.

The first participant read her vignette. As I remember, it was of the Puerto Rican home of her youth. Her quickly drafted, homey memories warmed all of us. She faced the woman next to her to indicate it was her turn. The woman looked at her paper and burst into tears. She tried to read a sentence or two, after which half the class started crying along with her. I quickly retrieved the boxes of tissues and passed them around. I certainly hadn't expected such a response. Although the woman couldn't continue, she later thanked me for the unexpected opening into something deep and painful and long-suppressed. Writing had helped release its power over her.

Regardless if our earthly experience of home is pleasant and safe or violent and chaotic, the idea of home strikes a strong chord in us. I wonder if we have an imprint on our souls that lingers, like a dream, just beyond our reach, of a place we know is safe and lovely and fulfills our longing to belong—a place we know as home. We once had a Samoyed when we lived in Vermont. They're those fluffy, white, curly-tailed dogs with coal black eyes and noses. They originally herded reindeer in Siberia. When the first blast of Arctic air blew in around November, Gus would lie in the yard all day, nose pointed right into the north wind, eyes partially closed. He looked as if he were trying to capture the scent of a memory of the place of his heritage drifting in on the wind.

The journey toward home is as ancient a literary image

as storytelling itself. The home goal for Jacob was the promised land of his fathers. But he did a lot of coming and going before he got there. He wandered off the trail, overstayed some of his visits, and side-tripped to places that got him in trouble. Because of his own misdeeds, he left his hometown as a man on the run. His plan was to head for safety at his uncle's home. Little did he know he was running right smack into the face of God.

The Lord encountered Jacob a half dozen times along his various journeys. Each time Jacob underwent another transformation, shedding a bit more of his earthy self. He left home with the shirt on his back; twenty years later he returned full of family, wealth, and a new heart for God. He had to wrestle an angel of the Lord all night before he got to the end of himself. When he begged a blessing, he received a new name—and a new identity.

He didn't get through unscathed though. The deceiver was in turn deceived and suffered from his own follies. But through it all, whether Jacob got into predicaments of his own making or not, God was working to transform a person and perform a purpose. He protected, provided, and ultimately delivered his traveler to the promised home, because getting sojourners home is his business.

Not even our mistakes can thwart his plans. There's a Jewish legend about a rabbi who noticed his daughter was sad. It was Sabbath eve, and she was responsible to light the Sabbath lamp. When her father asked what was wrong, she told him she'd mistaken the jar of vinegar for oil and had filled the lamp with it. "He replied, 'My daughter, why should you be concerned? He who ordained that oil should burn will ordain that even vinegar should burn.' The sages taught: Indeed, the lamp continued burning" (*The Book of Legends*, ed. Hayim Bialik and Yehoshua Ravnitzky).

Indeed, He who can keep the Sabbath lamp burning in spite of someone's mistake can fulfill the purpose and plan he has for me, in spite of my mine. I can take heart that the One who saw Jacob home will see me there too. To that final home. The forever one.

And I can promise Bob he won't have to do any renovations.

WORSHIP

ONE OF THE last things recorded about Jacob is that the self-reliant man who always had a plan, who got himself into dilemmas and tried to connive his way out, now, at the end of his days, bowed over his staff and worshiped. Worshiped the One who'd been guiding him all along.

4:30 a.m., the first day in our newly built house. We've been in the South for over a decade at this point. We have a brand-new home, two cars, and a dog in the yard. A refrigerator full of food and nice clothes on our backs. Bob has his workshop; I have a pool. We've had unexpected opportunities to express our gifts and talents along the way. But most important, we've seen the Lord walk with us through the dust, debris, and despair of our lives as surely as he has in the times of peace, beauty, and bounty.

I tiptoe out onto the wrap-around deck, snuggle down into the wicker rocker, and watch Orion, that celestial hunter, slide across the still dark sky. A cacophony of crickets surrounds me. A distant donkey brays, accompanied by an early-rising rooster from another direction. My thoughts circle back to the first word the Lord spoke to me: "Be still and know that I am God." My heart overflows with a good theme.

A sliver of light crests the horizon. I add my voice to this early morning chorus and worship the King.

ACKNOWLEDGMENTS

Will Rogers is purported to have said, "We can't all be heroes, because somebody has to sit on the curb and clap as they go by." I have many unsung heroes in my life. Here are a few I want to clap for this time around.

Carol Roper and *Beth Sadaati*, If we stopped meeting every other week, I don't think I'd dare publish another paragraph. Not only do I rely on the expertise you put into my words (even now I'm fretting that I can't have you critique this), but I cherish the encouragement, wisdom, and love you put into my life.

Lyn Riddle, Thank you for the chance you took on this fledgling writer and set her Southern saga spinning in a new direction. *Edie Melson* for the seemingly bottomless support and knowledge you so generously share. *Vie Herlocker*, for your eagle eye and obedient spirit. You were a real-time answer to a specific prayer.

And *Nancy Parker*, *Elizabeth C.*, *Tammy K.*, *Cathy B.*, *Lori R.*, and the women of the *Light Brigade*, my online accountability group, for the myriad of ways you've contributed your talents, friendships, and prayers over the years.

This is like making up a gift or guest list—you're sure to leave out someone special. But there are some whose stories are intrinsically intertwined in my own—*Scott*, when you were seven, we had a flat on a country road. I had no idea where the spare was in my new-to-me car. But you did. Always were and always will be someone I am proud of and can count on. *Nat*, Proverbs 31 voices the heart of many a mother—her children will rise up and call her blessed. I love sharing life with the lovely woman you've come to be. I am blessed.

Most of all—*Bob*—the same coming as going. Funny, inventive, passionate about the Lord. You supply my stories, enrich my life, and let me tell the world all about it.